And always Annaliese x

Learning to live with the death of our daughter

CLARE LOUISE

www.andalwaysannaliese.com

First paperback edition printed in
the United Kingdom, January 2023

Book and cover design by AnnMarie Reynolds for
begin a book Writing Services and Independent Publishers
www.beginabook.com

Cover image created by Annaliese;
adapted for digital publication by Lisa Williams

ISBN 978-1-915353-07-8 (Paperback)
ISBN 978-1-915353-08-5 (Hardback)

begin a book

www.beginabook.com

Dedication

For my children, with love, always and forever.

For Matt - my love, my best friend, an amazing Daddy – thank you for being you.

'Her absence is like the sky, it covers everything'

C S Lewis

Contents

Introduction

November 2021

You never think something like this is going to happen to you. Never. As a parent, you spend a lot of time worrying about your kids. Are they going to fall and bang their heads? Are they going to run into the road? Are they going to tumble down the stairs? Are they going to do well at school, get a good job, have a happy life? It never crosses your mind that one day they will have a runny nose and 48 hours later be in hospital receiving CPR.

CPR which is unsuccessful.

Yet this is what happened to my beautiful daughter Annaliese and to us, her family. Though it may not be an easy read at times it is our truth, our story and one which I genuinely believe for the sake of other families, is worth telling.

How this book works

I've chosen to write each section about a different aspect of my experience on purpose. You might want to skip to certain sections first and some may not be relevant to you, but the format is the same throughout. It is our story, what I've learnt and how others have helped us along the way.

How Did We Get Here?

Hello, I'm Clare, I'm in my early 50's and I'm an adoptive mother. I'm also a bereaved mother. Almost five years ago, our wonderful little girl died suddenly and unexpectedly. Annaliese's death changed the course of my life forever and her death is the reason I'm sharing our story. I hope that reading this will help you, whether you are a bereaved parent yourself or if you are trying to support someone whose child has died. Nothing prepares you for being a parent, and there's absolutely nothing that prepares you for the death of your child. The pain is unbearable and it feels like your world has stopped. The truth is that it does start again, but in a different way to before. Life as you knew it has changed forever. I've read many great books on grief over the years, but I wanted to tell our story – to make it something practical that might support you and your network. I think this would have been useful to me during those worst days of my life and I truly hope it helps you a little too.

Following several years of fertility issues and then a long intense adoption process, Annaliese came into our lives as a quiet, timid, and utterly gorgeous 18-month-old. We had waited a long time to be parents, and suddenly there we were, driving her home – excited to be her forever family. I remember that being one of the happiest times of my life – the joy of buying little wellies in Tesco, of hanging up a row of pink toddler clothes, of hearing her call me Mummy. As life continued (and her little brother came to join us a year later), we got caught up in the realities of family life with two small children. It was busy, tiring and at times tough. There's a good reason why parenting adopted children is described as 'parenting plus'. Adopted children have a layer of trauma in their lives by virtue of the fact they have been separated from their birth family. This often has an impact on how they develop, cope and behave. Parenting adopted children can require increased patience, resilience and understanding - perhaps more so than with birth children – hence its name. Nonetheless, we were happy and positive about our future together. A family of four. It was all we had ever wanted.

As the months ticked by (I wish I could casually say years, but we only got five years together), it became clear that Annaliese was a complicated little girl. She was highly anxious about many things in life, but also full of fun, mischief, and love. She was truly childlike in her approach and chatted away to animals ('Hello little fella') and stared with eyes full of wonder at Disney classics like Lady and the Tramp and The Jungle Book. She would sit for hours doing the same Frozen jigsaw puzzles over and over again, or explicitly follow the instructions for her Lego Cinderella carriage or Moana raft, and she would concentrate furiously over her colouring efforts - far more than any schoolwork, that's for sure! At the end of the school day, she would fling herself across the playground and into our arms - or someone else's. She was very generous with her affections, full of love, and squealed with delight when she was excited. She was our longed for little girl and we adored her.

I could write for days about her, in fact I must, because her brother was only five when Annaliese died, and I know he will struggle to remember all the funny little stories. How is it possible that he will have to read anecdotes about his big sister rather than grow up with her?

I wanted to write this book now because I have learned so much since Annaliese died. I've learned about grief and loss, about myself, about my relationship, about parenting a traumatised child, about friendship, and the most challenging lesson - carrying on with life. I wanted to write the book that would have been so helpful when our world fell apart. I wanted to write the book that I needed my family and friends to have at the time so they would understand better how to support us, how to understand our behaviour and how to accept the new (not improved) us. I wanted to offer you, the reader, hope – albeit only a glimmer at first, but hope, nonetheless. It's there somewhere, I promise, and I want to help you find it.

If you are reading this book, chances are that you, or someone you care about, is coping with this devastating experience, (or they may know it is coming). You could be a newly bereaved parent or you may have years of loss under your belt. For those who are newly bereaved, the pain of the loss never leaves, but you can learn to live alongside it. You may have lost your niece or nephew; or your friend, colleague or neighbour may have lost their child. Your reason for being here may be something else entirely, but you are all warmly welcomed.

I'm thinking of you as I write these words. I'm wrapping you in a warm hug and reassuring you that I understand.

You are safe within these pages. Take it at your own pace.

I've tried to make it simple to read. A book you can dip in and out of when you have the strength, and something you can navigate without too much effort. You have enough on your plate without wading through long, dense, and hard to read chapters. What you need right now is support, reassurance, acceptance and maybe even some advice. I promise you will find all that here. Losing someone you love is shit.

Losing your child ... is on another level entirely.

The First 48 Hours

On one hand it's quite hard to remember much about the first 48 hours, yet at the same time the moments are seared into my memory and heart forever. I try not to think about those days (though I often fail), the pain of them, the shock, the total loss of control. The day my life changed forever. Yet that time includes my precious last moments with Annaliese, the last cuddles, the last time I heard her say 'Mummy', the last time we were 'together'.

Obviously, all circumstances differ. We found ourselves in hospital that Friday morning, rushing there when we realised something was very wrong. We had been to the hospital the night before when we had first become concerned, but were discharged sometime later.

The following morning it was obvious Annaliese was not okay. She was very lethargic, her thighs were mottling, her lips were turning blue, so we scooped up our little girl and drove to the local hospital where just under three hours later she would die. I still can't get my head around that. We found out several days later that Annaliese had caught an infection (invasive group A streptococcus, also known as iGAS) which quickly led to sepsis. She died from multiple organ failure.

I won't detail those excruciating few hours, suffice to say it was distressing, scary, confusing, and utterly heart-breaking. It's what my diagnosis of *post-traumatic stress syndrome* is based on. When someone crouches in front of you and tells you he's 'sorry, we did everything we could but I'm afraid your daughter died a few moments ago', it's like an out of body experience. I remember making some sort of guttural, primeval moaning noise – I have no idea what it sounded like – and then we were ushered to a quiet corner, everyone looking at us with pity in their eyes, to be told what would happen next.

Annaliese was seven years old and her life had ended. It was incomprehensible. Somehow we managed to have conversations. We remembered our parking was about to run out – which the hospital took care of – and we spoke to the doctor who had overseen the emergency CPR. He sat next to me and explained more about what had happened to our beautiful daughter and for some inexplicable reason (that I'm still rather ashamed of), I told him how nice his aftershave smelt. I think I just couldn't believe what was happening was real and I was desperate to pretend this was a normal conversation.

Our son, who was five at the time, needed to be collected from school and brought into hospital too. The doctors were concerned the infection Annaliese caught might have been shared with both our son and us. Almost immediately we had to face the possibility that he could be heading in the same direction. It was too awful to contemplate.

I called a friend, told her what had happened and asked her to collect our son from school and bring him to us at the hospital. He arrived, bouncing around in his usual fashion and immediately asked where his sister was. We didn't tell him what had happened, instead we gently explained that Annaliese was in a different part of the hospital and that we needed him to have a few tests.

Looking back, I simply don't know how we functioned, but the incredible thing is that you do. You just put one foot in front of the other. You are in the most unexpected crisis management scenario of your life and so you make decisions moment by moment, focusing only on what is needed at that time.

For us, we turned our attentions to our little boy whilst still trying to process that Annaliese had just died. I remember feeling like it wasn't true, even though I was making phone calls to tell our closest family and friends. My sister drove straight to the hospital to be with us. I remember walking down a corridor to meet her and sobbing in her arms. In some strange way I felt like I was acting, that it wasn't possible, that at some point we would get back to normal. I was in shock. It's a powerful emotion which stayed with me for days.

The hours that followed Annaliese's death are a bit of a blur. We had to spend the night in hospital with our son so he could be monitored. We curled up, clinging to one another on a camp bed and quietly sobbed, trying not to disturb our boy. I recall getting up and calling my friend Kate at around 3am. I will always remember her kindness, just being there to listen to me cry. There wasn't much to be said - I simply didn't want to be alone. The next day we were allowed home as outpatients and were monitored for the following week, having to return to the hospital several times. I remember walking into our house and feeling uncomfortable. It didn't feel like a safe space because Annaliese wasn't there. All her things were there, as they had been the day before, but she wasn't ever going to see them again.

Even aged five, our son clearly knew something wasn't right. There were people coming and going. Mummy and Daddy were really sad. And his big sister was nowhere to be seen. We were terrified of telling him and struggled to know when the right time would be to explain the truth. Two days after Annaliese's death, our friend Alex (a fellow parent with daughters in both our kids' classes) persuaded us gently but firmly, that we should talk to him right now, like in the next ten minutes. I'm not sure I would ever have felt ready. Alex waited outside our front door to give us some privacy but she was right there afterwards to support us in whatever way we needed. What happened next is one of my most painful memories. We sat our little boy between us at the kitchen table and said, 'You know how Annaliese wasn't feeling very well the other day …?'

'She's dead isn't she?' he hurriedly asked. Just like that. He knew. My heart shattered as he sobbed in my arms and blubbered, 'I want my sister back'.

It was one of the hardest things I'd ever had to do and now, almost five years on, the pain and loss he feels is something I still find hard to bear.

I remember not wanting to be alone in the house, just the three of us, so we gave keys to a few friends who took shifts being with us those first few days. They cooked, they tidied, they played with our son when we needed time to ourselves. They gave him baths, read bedtime stories, arranged the vases and vases of flowers which kept on arriving and stacked the *'sorry for your loss'* cards that spilled through the letterbox. The postman asked my partner if it was someone's special birthday because there were so many cards. He was mortified when he learned the real reason.

What have I learnt?

That I'm stronger than I realised. That when the worst possible thing I could have imagined happened, I managed to remain upright, have conversations, think about what needed to be done next. I still don't know how I did those things in hindsight, but I think you go into some sort of automatic pilot.

What can your support crew do to help?

- Take care of practical things – make sure meals are cooked, washing up is done, flowers are put in vases and watered, cancel any appointments you have that you now can't attend, take on the 'mental load' of running a household, and just be there. We were guided by our support team on so many aspects of what had to happen next. We weren't sleeping much and couldn't think clearly for ourselves. They sorted out a funeral director and arranged a meeting with her at our house. They liaised with the school and organised for the Headmistress and Deputy Head to come and see us. They gave me a list of bereavement support services/groups and booked us an appointment to see our GP. I remember an old schoolfriend who didn't even know our kids, sending me a delivery of children's books about loss/death so that we could read our son some suitable stories. It was such a kind and practical thing to do.

- Whilst flowers are nice, our house ended up looking like a florist. I didn't have enough vases; I was giving bunches of flowers away.

In my experience, receiving a 'care parcel' was really helpful. We had an amazing package delivered that kept us in food for a couple of weeks. Friends also left meals they'd made for us on the doorstep. About a month afterwards, friends who were based in Dubai at the time, sorted out a Waitrose grocery delivery with lovely carefully chosen items – and even included a cuddly camel for our son! This meant we didn't need to think about food shopping for about a month and it REALLY helped because frankly, we didn't have the headspace for it. Everything doesn't have to arrive within 48 hours of the tragedy – in fact, it's better to space it out. As well as running out of vases, freezer space became a challenge too. A neighbour that we didn't really know left a tray of fairy cakes that she'd made especially for our son. It was a thoughtful act of kindness and made him feel special.

- Within half an hour of Annaliese's death, our friends Gemma and Alex picked our son up from school, delivered him to us at the hospital and then at the end of the day (it was a Friday before a half term), drove round and spoke to every single one of Annaliese's classmates' parents to explain what had happened.

As I think about that now I am overwhelmed at what an upsetting thing that must have been to do. We still find telling people what happened very painful – so having others to take care of it for us in the early days really helped.

- I felt compelled to get some totally unnecessary (in hindsight) things sorted – I think it was my brain trying to exert some control during a time when I felt I had none. About a week before Annaliese died I'd bought her a big stack of new clothes for the summer in anticipation of our first family holiday abroad. Immediately after her death I had this overwhelming urge to take them back to the shop – I couldn't bear seeing them - so Alex took them off my hands and sorted it out. She did a lot of that, and I felt so grateful to let someone take care of whatever I needed at that moment. Alex was also sensitive about her own daughter being in the same space as us as she is one of Annaliese's classmates. At the time it was very hard for me to be around other seven-year-old little girls. I've learned to cope with that (mostly) but having others understand the impact of those kind of situations, really made a difference.

The Funeral

Planning your child's funeral is simply wrong. We all know it shouldn't be this way around, yet that was exactly what we were faced with. Our funeral director was a wonderfully sensitive lady called Gill. She had been recommended by our friend Claire who had lost her young god-daughter years before and so had some heartbreakingly valuable experience. Gill sat with us at our large kitchen table and took us through the next steps and decisions we needed to make. Casket, burial or cremation? How many attendees? What did we want her to wear on her final journey? I have a vivid memory of taking Annaliese's powder blue Cinderella ballgown off a little plastic hanger, picking out some small flowery knickers and insisting on a vest too because the dress always made her feel itchy. I put the clothes in a plastic bag and gave them to Gill so that once her body had been collected from the hospital, they could tenderly dress Annaliese in them. I can feel a physical reaction just typing those words; my breathing has slowed, my legs feel heavy, and my heart feels bruised and sore. The agony of that moment will last the rest of my lifetime.

We quickly recognised we were in very safe hands. Gill was so kind, telling us there was no charge - other than the crematorium fees, which fell outside of her jurisdiction. I wept at this sort of kindness. It took some of the financial burden away but with every kind gesture flung our way (and there were plenty), it reminded me how enormous our tragedy was. Everyone was gentle with us, everyone wanted to help, and everyone was bloody thankful it wasn't them. I remember our window cleaner was there when we met with the funeral director and he wouldn't take any money either.

It's often said that planning the funeral at least gives you something to focus on and I found that to be true. At the time we, particularly me, just flicked into action mode. We had to plan the service, choose photos and words, sort flowers, write a eulogy (we had a wonderful celebrant who read it for us) and trawl through hours of video clips so that we could put together a montage to play on the day. The idea of doing this now makes me feel panicky. I regularly look at photos, but videos are harder. Annaliese is so real and alive; I can hear her voice and see all those little expressions that I miss so much. At the time however, I think I was just on automatic pilot. It had to be done, we had a deadline and we wanted to make everything the best we possibly could to honour our beautiful daughter. When the video montage was played at the funeral I dissolved into loud, ugly sobs the moment it started. I kept my eyes firmly fixed forward during the whole service and didn't really 'see' anyone else there – but I'm told that the tears flowed freely for many.

The lead up to the day itself was intensely painful. I felt total fear about facing the day – particularly about seeing everyone who would be there. We had been in a little bubble for three weeks, only allowing the inner circle of incredible friends in. The thought of seeing over 100 people made me feel sick. We knew all eyes would be on us, of course with love and support, but still … it was the biggest, heaviest black cloud of our lives hanging over us.

Before that though, we had another big decision to make. Did we want to see Annaliese in the funeral parlour? Our immediate reaction was that we didn't, we wanted to remember her skipping around the place rather than laying in a casket. This is the most personal of decisions and I'm acutely aware some parents don't even get this opportunity based on the circumstances. We discussed it at length and in the end changed our minds. The idea of being with her just one last time was too tempting and irrationally we didn't want to 'let her down' by not going. We had just about got our heads around it when the funeral director told us that due to Annaliese's cause of death she was somewhat discoloured, and that we should prepare ourselves for that. Yet again we were thrown into a quandary as to what to do. It was at this moment that three amazingly brave and kind friends from the inner sanctum offered to go and see Annaliese on our behalf. They would then tell us whether they thought it would be a good idea for us to visit. The three of them left our house and were back within half an hour, quiet and looking intensely sad. They all agreed it would be better if we didn't see Annaliese like that (which is making me cry just typing it) – so that's how it was decided. I'm forever grateful to them for being prepared to do that for us. We heeded their advice and though we still chose to visit her, we asked for the casket to remain closed. Sitting in a small, dimly lit room with her beautiful wicker casket in front of us was yet another out of body experience. You simply can't believe you are in this situation. That your little seven-year-old blonde-haired munchkin is in there wearing her favourite Cinderella dress. We talked to her, tears streaming down our faces, about how much we had loved being her parents, how much happiness and fun she'd brought to our family and how much we were going to miss her.

I think we stayed about an hour but in all honesty I have no idea. I do remember that before we left I stood with my hands on top of the casket and sung her the bedtime lullaby I would sing to her every night when I put her to bed. And then we left, returned home, sat with our friends around the kitchen table and fell apart for a little while. The intensity of the emotions you experience at a time like this is extraordinary and the exhaustion is intense. I think that's one of the side effects of grief that's impossible to understand until you are in it. The sheer fatigue of coping with it all can be debilitating. One of the things that I make sure I do now is get enough sleep. Without it, I'm quickly a mess again.

We had asked to keep locks of her hair which I sometimes get out of the box and sniff just to feel close again. Recently I told our son about this and he wanted to see them straight away. I explained one of the boxes was for him if he wanted it, and we both looked at this beautiful blonde hair with a gentle curl in it. It was a very tender, moving moment. One thing I wished I had thought to ask the funeral director, was for them to take finger and toe prints. I would love some jewellery made from those. I only thought about it a few months after the funeral though which was, of course, too late.

And so, the funeral day arrived, a beautifully sunny Friday in June – totally incongruous with what was going to be happening. At 7.30am a friend collected our son and took him to his weekly football club before school which left us with four hours or so to wait until the funeral director arrived to pick us up. We made the decision not to take our son to the funeral. Again, this is a very personal choice, but at five years old we felt he was too young, and we knew that we would be extremely emotional and upset and didn't want him to see us like that. Selfishly I wanted to be able to express my emotions freely without worrying about the impact on him. My usually calm partner had a panic attack as he was getting ready to go, and I scrabbled around to find a paper bag for him to blow into as he sat on the side of the bed. It all felt like a bad dream.

I spent around two hours on the phone to another good friend, Lyndon, who had been an enormous support emotionally. This was someone I'd lived with at university and he knew me very well. He was also straight talking and rational and was the kind of friend I could call in the middle of the night when I couldn't sleep. He would just listen and tell me I would be okay. That morning I told him I didn't think I could face the funeral and that I would fall apart. Lyndon gently but firmly reassured me that I *would* be able to face it and that however I behaved was totally okay – no one was expecting anything of me. All I had to think about, he said, was getting through it for the two of us and for Annaliese. Eventually he had to hang up so that he could get to the crematorium in time. I really needed him that morning and I will never forget how he helped me.

After what felt like the longest morning of our lives, eventually we found ourselves in the chapel. We had chosen for Annaliese to already be there waiting – I couldn't cope with seeing her being taken out of the back of a hearse. We were alone with our daughter for the very last time. We arrived through a back door and were already sitting down facing forwards as the chapel began to fill up. In truth, I have little recollection of who was there. We faced forwards, clung on to our chairs and each other for dear life. It was a beautiful service, full of music that she loved, gorgeous photos, video clips and bursting with love. Just as she deserved.

When the time came to leave, we wanted to escape quickly. Again, we had pre-arranged to leave the chapel first with friends who were driving us to a pub for the wake. I couldn't make eye contact with anyone; I knew I would shatter into a thousand pieces if I did. So, I glanced over at the casket, held Matt's hand tightly and told our little girl I loved her before dashing out of the door. The relief that it was done felt overwhelming. I cried as we walked to the car. It just didn't feel like this could possibly be my life.

The wake was surreal. All our family and friends, on a beautiful sunny afternoon in a pub garden - it felt like a celebration, which in some ways it was, yet it wasn't. I surprised myself by being able to have a few drinks, even a gentle laugh with people I hadn't seen for ages. Later in the afternoon a handful of children arrived. We chose not to have children at the service, but we had agreed with a couple of close friends that their kids would come, with our son, to the pub once school had finished. We told him that everyone was here to remember all the love they have for Annaliese and, aged five, he accepted that and played with his pals in the pub garden. It was both lovely and horrendous at the same time.

One thing that I'm sure is very common is on the day following the funeral, we were utterly exhausted. We had willed ourselves to face that day, got through it and then… the rest of our lives without Annaliese stretched ahead. I felt jet lagged, battered, bruised and deeply sad. Friends came over and brought lunch for us all with them, so I didn't have to think about a thing. We went for a walk in the local park with their dog. I felt like I was in a daze and just going through the motions really, but it was nice not to be alone and to have a distraction. I'm sure it wasn't easy to be with us that day, but they put caring for us before their discomfort and I'm forever grateful for that. It took us almost two years to be able to have her ashes at home. They stayed in the funeral parlour all that time and whilst I felt guilty, I just wasn't ready. Then, one day, the lovely funeral director came back to our house holding a large paper bag with colourful cord handles which contained a box of ashes. That is another moment you never think you are going to have to face. Carrying that bag upstairs felt utterly devastating, each step heavy and exhausting. We still can't decide what to do with her ashes so they remain tucked away at the back of our wardrobe surrounded by some of her favourite cuddly toys. It's a very personal thing and there are no rules about this sort of stuff. You simply do what feels right for you, your family, and your child. If you feel there is judgement from others about your choice, you must push past that – it's not their decision. They are not living with that loss in the way that you are. You do what you need to do.

What have I learnt?

Having practical things to focus on helped me to keep going. I couldn't crumple completely, I had to make sure it was right for our girl. It gave Matt and I a shared objective, we didn't think about what came after her funeral – we just focused on getting to that day.

People are kind. There were so many thoughtful and lovely things that they did for us in the run up to the funeral and on the day itself. It's hard not to find that overwhelming at times, but it's obvious that others really do want to help and will try their best to look after you.

What can your support crew do to help?

- Recommend a funeral director. A personal recommendation/introduction was one less thing to fret about and having someone else attend the meetings with us was also extremely helpful. Our minds were very unreliable at that point and having another person there made it less stressful.

- Listen to what your friend or family member wants and respect their wishes. Ensure the wider circle of friends and family do the same. Whatever approach they want to take for their child's funeral is all that matters and as the support crew, you can manage any 'noise' from others around this.

- Help with the practical things if you can. We are lucky enough to have a friend who is a printer so he and his wife came to see us, asked what we wanted for the Order of Service and prepared something truly beautiful. I was incredibly touched at the care and attention he showed in doing that for us. My younger sister Beth took care of sorting out a lovely guest book where people were able to write little stories of their memories of Annaliese.

On the day she was the one who made sure people were writing in it and it's something we will always treasure.

- I've already mentioned the friends who provided our 'getaway' car – they were also the ones to go and pick our son up from school and bring him to the pub. Is this what it feels like to be famous? Having people run around taking care of things like this for you? It felt uncomfortable and we wished that we didn't need the help - even though we were very grateful for it.

Coping with An Inquest and Handling Medical Negligence

Thankfully, this is not something that every bereaved parent will have to go through. There are, of course, other scenarios where you will need to deal with the police, the media or even authorities in another country. For us we faced an inquest in the United Kingdom followed by a medical negligence case against the NHS. Whilst your experience might be with a different authority or country, I hope some of the things I've learnt might come in useful. Hence the inclusion of this chapter.

I'm not going to go into specific details, but I can talk about the experience of having to find a solicitor, preparing for and attending an inquest, and making the decision to bring a case against our local NHS Trust.

The case we brought was for medical negligence and we also reported a couple of specific doctors to the General Medical Council. We wanted to hold them to account for the decisions they made in the course of their care of our daughter.

Initially, when Annaliese died, we were told by the hospital it was an unavoidable tragedy – just one of those random and cruel things that can happen which no one could have done anything about. In the early days of total shock, with a brain that was capable of very little cognitive thought, we readily accepted that explanation.

However, because Annaliese was so young and had died so suddenly in hospital, our local NHS Health Trust was duty bound to conduct a serious incident report investigation and share the findings with us. I will never forget receiving that report and sitting at my kitchen table reading it about three months after she had died. The words on the page made it clear – protocol wasn't followed, opportunities to potentially save her were missed.

The enormity of that possibility crushed us once more. It was devastating to imagine our sweet, innocent little girl might have died because of medical negligence. We found it almost impossible to wrap our heads around that scenario.

We have a couple of friends with extensive NHS and medical experience and their support at that time really helped us. With their guidance we were able to better understand the information we had been sent (the report) and work out what questions we should be asking.The consultant from the hospital assigned to deal with us at this stage was someone I'd known for a few years. She had been seeing Annaliese regularly to review her childhood absence epilepsy. She was someone I'd grown to trust and liked and I wanted to believe her when she told me, '*Sometimes these things just happen,*' but the truth was, we had been let down by a series of errors made by a few medical professionals. When you have the chance to pick over every detail minute by minute, you quickly see any cracks in the care your child received. These cracks were obvious once we had received and studied the report and for us, it felt important that the hospital and the team involved in Annaliese's care that night, were held to account. Our daughter had died, potentially unnecessarily, and we wanted to make sure that lessons were learnt so that no other family would experience what we were living through.

We decided to find a solicitor and get some advice about whether they thought we had a case of negligence to bring against the local NHS Health Trust. We also wanted to know if we would need representation at the inquest, which was yet to be scheduled.

We couldn't afford to spend a lot of money and quickly realised that a 'no win, no fee' approach would be best for us. Not knowing where to start, we did a local Google search and I asked the solicitor I'd used for house moves and wills for some advice. He told me about a big city law firm that were very experienced in medical negligence and well thought of. Once we had contacted them, we quickly felt we were in safe hands.

If you find yourselves needing a lawyer, I'd recommend talking with two or three people. You will likely find that you 'click' with one more than the others, and that's an important factor. You need someone you can communicate easily with and that you trust implicitly.

Our chosen solicitor became yet another person that we had to share our story with, in intricate detail. I remember phone conversations replaying the last 48 hours of our daughter's life. It was emotional and upsetting, but the solicitor was patient and professional. To begin with she reviewed the facts to decide whether the case was one they (and us) were likely to win. When she confirmed that they would take on our case, another tiny piece of my heart broke. It was confirmation that mistakes had indeed been made and that we had every right to demand 'justice'. Whatever that means though, it will never bring our daughter back.

This all happened about six months after Annaliese died, and it took almost four years to reach a settlement agreement with the NHS. It can take forever, and you need to have a fair amount of resolve and grim determination to keep going. Our solicitor told me that NHS solicitors sometimes drag their feet in the hope that people get so battle weary, they give up. Knowing that only made me more determined to see our case through and ensure that lessons would be learnt and processes amended, so no other families find themselves in our position.

The painful truth is that families face this every single day. Around 48,000 people a year die from sepsis (Sepsis UK Trust) and in many cases, the signs are not picked up early enough. Anything we could do to raise awareness and hold the 'system' to account felt right. The day we finally concluded the negotiations was emotionally brutal. I felt a wave of relief, anger and sadness knock me off my feet. Approaching the fourth anniversary of Annaliese's death, I was looking at a number on an email that was 'compensation' for our girl's life. It was painful, upsetting and felt like the end of a chapter. On the one hand I was relieved this part of it was all over, but on the other it felt as if I was closing a door I'd never wanted to open.

I have only positive things to say about the experience with our legal firm. They made this extraordinarily painful process as gentle as they could. Our solicitor was straight talking and good at her job. She was always respectful and tried to minimise the pressure on us to furnish her with details, review reports, agree next steps etc … whilst keeping the case moving forwards.

Once we had the legal support alongside us, our first big hurdle was to get through the inquest. Not every bereaved parent has to face this thank goodness, but many do, and I found the thought of it utterly terrifying.

Whilst we were trying to decide which legal firm to hire, one solicitor told us that we didn't really need anyone to represent us at the inquest but they'd spring into action once the ruling from the inquest was made. Conversely, the firm we engaged believed having a solicitor and a barrister at the inquest was essential. How right they were. Having lived through the experience I couldn't imagine being there without the professional guidance and advice they were able to provide. Both our solicitor and barrister had experience of medical negligence cases, and this was invaluable.

Navigating anything to do with the NHS is a challenge – though I would like to make it clear that I recognise how lucky we are to have the NHS and that there are many, many times when they make the most incredible, positive difference to someone's care. It's just for us, on that fateful day, they didn't make that incredible, positive difference, and now I'm writing a book about the loss of my seven-year-old daughter who could possibly have been saved. Had she received the correct medical care at the right time, the outcome would likely have been different. These days, I have a very conflicted relationship with the NHS and I found it hard during the pandemic to offer the waves of love and admiration that many did. My grieving mind whispered, *'but my daughter isn't here because of them'*, and that was hard to ignore.

Without the insights of my school friend Louise and the experience and expertise of our legal team in the run up to and during the two-day inquest, I am sure some details that came to light would have remained unseen. Although it was horrendous to revisit the minutiae of the details, we both felt it was our responsibility to insist that every decision taken in regard to Annaliese's care was examined carefully. Nothing could be done to bring her back, but we were determined to uncover the truth about her medical care and the devastating consequences.

Attending your child's inquest is immensely painful and upsetting. I focused several sessions of EMDR (Eye Movement Desensitisation and Reprocessing) therapy on the inquest so that I would be able to sit and listen to the details without shattering into a million pieces. My therapist gave me practical things to do and focus on whilst we sat in the coroner's court. She recommended I take a packet of mints to suck on when I felt particularly panicked (the idea being that the act of focusing on something else – the unwrapping of the packet, the taste, the feel of the mint with a hole on my tongue – would distract my brain just enough to remain seated rather than be a wailing heap on the floor). I took Bach's remedy rescue, one of Annaliese's little cuddly toys (a tiny kitten which I could hold unobtrusively in my hand, bring to my face and smell when I needed it) and lots of tissues. As the inquest approached I felt sick with anxiety and fear – but I told myself that I'd already faced the worst day of my life, so this was nothing by comparison. I relied on my therapy survival strategies, the expertise of our legal team, the love of my partner and the support of four amazing friends who sat alongside us for the duration.

I found, as is often the case, that the anticipation of the inquest was worse than the experience itself, though it was still distressing, painful and utterly heart-breaking. Once we were there, in the moment, sitting at a table in the coroner's court surrounded by our friends and legal team, I managed to find the strength to get through each minute, and then the next and then the next. We didn't learn anything during the inquest that we didn't already know but hearing the intricate detail of her last 18 hours felt like someone was piercing irreparable holes in my heart. It was incredibly difficult to be in the same room as the medical staff I'd seen on that day – some of whom had taken the decision not to follow the process they should have, which likely contributed to our daughter's death. It's impossible to explain what it feels like hearing them give their account of things, and having the chance to look them in the eye and watch their body language was a real challenge. It was obvious that a few of them felt very emotional and one student doctor who had been involved on both visits we made in that short time became upset and tearful as he recounted his version of events. I've since learned that he moved to Australia and went into a different area of medicine. Conversely, another doctor who made a critical decision early on which impacted everything that followed, was cold, robotic and didn't even look at us. It felt as if she'd been advised by her legal counsel to behave the way she did and I found it unforgiveable, inhumane, and disrespectful.

The inquest was eventually over and the coroner, who was amazing throughout, summed up his thoughts based on everything he'd heard. In a coroner's court there is no 'guilty' or 'not guilty' verdict, it's about establishing the facts, but there is certainly an undercurrent of what was right and what was not right. We left the inquest knowing that our girl had been failed by the doctors and professionals whose job it was to keep her alive.

What have I learnt?

- Humans are resilient. There have been a few times in my life when I've thought I couldn't do something - Annaliese's funeral and inquest are numbers one and two - but despite my fear and dread, I did manage to get through them.

- It's important to have the right professionals and people supporting you whether that's a therapist, solicitor, a friend with expertise in the area or someone that can simply hold your pain and just be by your side.

- You must be patient and determined when it comes to inquests and legal proceedings. We were relatively 'lucky' - the inquest took place 10 months after Annaliese died. I know many others who have waited much longer than this.

- I've learnt to navigate medical and legal reports. Keeping on top of the facts was important to me, despite the pain I felt every time I read those documents.

What can your support crew do to help?

- If you have professional experience that relates to the nature of death or the circumstances around it, then please offer to share your knowledge and opinions with those affected. At a time when their brains will be operating at a much lower capacity than normal, you can really make a difference.

- As always, suspend judgement. I know there are people who thought our continuing legal proceedings were detrimental to our wellbeing. 'It won't bring Annaliese back,' they would say, and 'won't it just cause more distress?' Whilst both of those points are true, it felt extremely important to us that the people who made the decisions on that day, and in particular those who did not follow the correct process, were held to account. I can't really explain this (and I don't need to), but people's gentle questioning around why we were pushing through with legal proceedings, didn't feel helpful.

- If you are a close friend or family member and you feel able, offer to attend the inquest in a support role. You may not be needed but offering is a kind and selfless thing to do. Personally, we found it very valuable having a few close friends with us. It made us feel less isolated, more loved, and protected. Also, extra pairs of ears to listen to what's being said is advisable. It's hard to take in everything when you are flooded with raw emotion.
- If you are in the wider circle of friends/family, try to appreciate that the lead up to an inquest is an incredibly stressful and upsetting time for the parents so you need to treat them with kindness and understanding. Let them know you are thinking of them and their child(ren). If you want to do something practical, you could prepare a meal for them the night before and during the inquest. We, for example, had no energy for anything other than survival during those days.

Secondary Losses

This is something I wasn't really prepared for. It's not something that occurs to you until you experience it. I naively thought that the hardest aspect of my new reality would be missing Annaliese. The truth is, whilst that is obviously the biggest part, there are many other losses which revealed themselves over the months and years following her death. Being totally honest (even though it sounds a little dramatic) there isn't <u>any</u> aspect of my life now that isn't impacted by Annaliese's death. Everything is different now. Here's a brain dump of those 'secondary losses' that immediately come to mind:

- All my relationships feel changed in some way. I'm a different person, so therefore all my relationships are different. People find talking about death hard, people find talking about the death of a child impossible and so they don't (mostly).

- The family dynamics in both our household and with wider family aren't the same, and whilst we still live in the same house, sleep in the same bedrooms, watch the same TV on the same sofas, somehow, everything is affected by Annaliese not being here.

- The future we imagined – not finishing primary school, not getting to double figures of age (I still remember the excitement of turning 10), not getting to wear the 'these will fit next year' clothes I'd bought for her which were sitting in the drawer untouched, not picking her up from parties or discos, not seeing her learn to drive, not seeing her fall in love then comforting her when it all went wrong, not going wedding dress shopping with her, not seeing her become a mother – in that moment, we had lost all of this and much, much more.

- My confidence – realising that I was not in control of anything, my confidence packed up and left me for a couple of years.

- My career – see above, no confidence = a very different approach to work.

- No longer having my daughter in my life – I miss the things that meant a lot to us both, the love of Disney (Cinderella, Lady and the Tramp, Snow White and the Seven Dwarfs), the amount of pink in our lives, listening to showtunes, snuggling up and watching endless repeats of Strictly together, doing her hair. When Frozen 2 came out I thought my heart would literally explode with pain. Now she will never see that film and I can't bring myself to watch it without her.

- The impact on our son and therefore us, is HUGE. Seeing him cope with the loss of his sister has been excruciatingly hard, particularly when we ourselves are in a place of deep grief. If he was just sad and needed comfort, love, and support, that would be one thing to deal with. The reality is, as well as being sad, he's scared, angry, frustrated, lonely, confused, aggressive and very vulnerable. It's like the worst double whammy as a parent and we've had to dig deep, and still are, to cope with supporting him the way he needs. Throw in a global pandemic and that's been the reality of 2020/2021 for us.

- The places we don't go anymore. I think our son found it really painful going somewhere that we used to visit as a family of four, and so very quickly our routines became different. In some ways this was good for all of us, but I really miss the familiarity of being in the places Annaliese was happy, for example the Christmas Panto that lots of school families go to. That's something we just don't do anymore.
- The music. Annaliese loved listening to the soundtracks from her favourite films and until very recently there were a stack of CDs next to the little CD player on the desk in her room. She would ask me to leave my phone in the bathroom when she showered and have it play the soundtrack from Oliver! She used to belt out her rendition of Nancy's classic 'It's a fine life' with huge drama. It was both beautiful and hilarious. I used to tell her that one day I would watch her on stage when she was performing that song and I'd say to everyone, *'That's my daughter singing, isn't she amazing?'* Annaliese would look at me wide eyed at the very idea this was a possibility. It's a gorgeous memory tinged with sadness, as they all are.

- Mother's Day. For weeks before Mother's Day you are bombarded with advertising, emails, and social media posts. I try to ignore it, delete the emails, turn the page of a newspaper over, change the TV or radio channel. On the day itself, my wonderful other half does his best to make me feel loved and appreciated but there's no denying it's a tough day. We don't go out for a special lunch anywhere – who, in our situation, wants to eat surrounded by happy families? We choose to have a quiet day at home instead. I've learnt to lower my expectations in terms of my son's behaviour too. I think he finds days like Mother's Day and my birthday hard to cope with. He is often distant with me, almost angry and I think he feels the pressure of being the only child left to make a fuss, which for him is too much. Mother's Day is a day we let pass without considerable difference from any other Sunday.

What have I learnt?

- That missing her is just one part of the loss that I feel.

- That life is irrevocably changed, and I have to learn to live with that somehow.

- Acceptance is the path that will take me as near to happiness as I can get, but finding that acceptance is much harder than it sounds. Lowering your expectations can be helpful. It may sound defeatist but in fact it's very liberating.

- I also think it's helpful to recognise that it's totally okay to free yourself from the pressure of how you've always done things before, or what other people might expect you to do. This is your path, get comfortable with following your instincts when it comes to how much you can cope with, whatever the circumstances.

What can your support crew do to help?

- If secondary losses are a surprise to the bereaved parent, then they rarely occur to your support network. My best advice, if you are supporting someone who has lost a child, is to think proactively of the times of year that are likely to be hard e.g., birthdays, anniversaries, Mother's and Father's Day, Christmas, holidays, start of a new school year, and remember to acknowledge that with them. Send a message or card and mention their child's name – I can't stress this point enough. Phone them and leave a message if they don't answer, drop a bunch of flowers on the doorstep. That first year is particularly brutal of course, but don't forget those dates are going to be hard for them every year.

- Keep an open mind. What seems difficult for them may seem like nothing to you, but you aren't living with their grief, so refrain from judging and do your best to listen if they want to talk or give support in whichever way feels most appropriate for them.

Friends & Family

I think death can bring out the best and the worst reactions in people. And the death of a child seems to heighten either reaction. In the immediacy after Annaliese dying, we were surrounded by people, all being exceptionally kind and supportive. Taking care of us like we were wounded birds. For the first week or so our kitchen always had friends in it which I found comforting - I feared this changed reality with just the three of us. It felt like a new pair of shoes that I didn't choose or want; uncomfortable and unfamiliar.

Friends fell into a kind of rota where someone was with us in the evenings during the first couple of weeks to make us dinner and help put our son to bed, as well as just being there whilst we talked through the necessary plans that we had to make. You will be amazed at how much people want to help. One friend in particular, Louise, made the effort to come with us to meetings at the hospital and attended the inquest as well. I hadn't seen her for years and she'd never met Matt before, yet she selflessly guided and helped, and for her support we are forever thankful.

I guess the point is that your friends and family are likely to surprise you – some of them will surpass any expectations you ever had and some will fall short. I've learned over the years that the key is to lower your expectations. That may sound negative, but it's honest. I've no doubt that everyone felt for us and thought about us during that time, but many were unable to turn those feelings and thoughts into an action that helped. Death is a subject which for many is awkward, painful, and sad. Imagine that death is sudden and is of a beautiful blonde seven-year-old little girl – it's hard to know what to do with that isn't it?

Our experience was that our world shrank very quickly to include just a few people who were able to cope with the new versions of us. We were in a place of deep shock, extreme sadness, anger and living with profound grief. We had less capacity to take others' feelings into consideration at that stage - it was all we could do to concentrate on taking care of our young son and putting one foot in front of the other. I'm sure it wasn't easy being alongside us at that point.

Some found the patience and strength to be there, and some didn't. From conversations I've had with other bereaved parents, I've learned that's a common experience. Your own family in particular seem to struggle to support you. They are going through their own grief at losing a family member, and I think being faced with our (your) pain and tunnel vision (focusing on our son and survival), was just too hard for them to cope with. Your family desperately want you back the way you were before and can find it hard to understand that's not going to happen. This change in dynamics has caused me a lot of angst over the years but is something I'm now starting to come to terms with.

Until recently I was so caught up in a spiral of grief, I couldn't comprehend that people weren't able to instinctively know what I needed. I felt abandoned, let down and at times angry. Time, however, has helped me gain some perspective. I know people don't set out to hurt or offend, it's simply that few had the understanding or emotional capacity to cope with what we were facing, and so it felt easier to stand back and give us space. This reaction was, in fact, the opposite of what we needed – but they didn't know that.

I've tried to be open about grief and loss over the years - sometimes face to face, sometimes on social media. Many friends have made contact to thank me for my honesty and the resources I have shared. They feel it's helped them to understand what we were and are going through, and now feel able to support others they know in a more insightful and practical way. That's the point of this book – to pass on what I've learnt from our experiences in order to reassure you that what you are feeling is normal.

I want to tell you that you are not alone and to encourage you to keep taking it one step at a time. I also want to give you hope that you will find a way to live alongside the pain which will be your constant companion. I expect there are also friends who feel I'm too focused on my grief, that I should try and only remember the good times with Annaliese - which is so easy to say but not easy to do. The openness I have around my grief can make others feel a little uncomfortable I think. I'm very quick to talk about Annaliese and have never shied away from using the words dead or death. I know others feel differently and as I've said before, it's a very personal experience. If you can't face those words then that's absolutely okay. For me though, it felt right to use factual language.

What have I learnt?

- That people will surprise you – in both a good and a bad way. Those who have held me up (figuratively speaking) are not necessarily the ones I would have expected. This realisation has caused me much sadness, but the truth is, you need to take the support, kindness, and love where you find it, not where you think it should be.

- I've come to truly love the friends who have accepted whatever version of me they find on any given day. They are the ones that remember (and mention) the important days. They talk to me about Annaliese, some have photos of her in their houses because they miss her too. They keep the memory of her alive with their children, some of whom are Annaliese's friends, because they want her to be talked about. These friends instinctively understand that she was here, she lived, she mattered, and they care as much about our son as they do about us. They are interested in how he's coping, how they can support and they make time to connect with him and help him feel safe. That's a precious gift to us and is slowly allowing our son to heal too.

- It's taken some time, but with the help of therapy, I'm slowly finding the capacity to accept that some people haven't been able to do this for us. I know deep down that they didn't mean to cause me more pain or to contribute to the isolation I've felt. I've come to understand that it's common for many to be uncomfortable around the new life we have now. I've realised there is no benefit in carrying anger. It serves no purpose and so letting it go is what I'm aiming for.

What can your support crew do to help?

- Be there. Be patient, be kind, be understanding and don't judge how your bereaved friend or family member may be behaving. Unless you are also a bereaved parent, you really don't get what's going on for them.

- Talk to them about their child. Share stories, send photos that you have of them (a photo that I've never seen of her before is such a precious gift to me now). Have it firmly in your mind that their child is still a part of their family and still a part of their everyday life. Though that might seem strange to you and may make you a little uncomfortable, that doesn't matter - it's not about you, it's about them. There have been several occasions when parents of children in Annaliese's class have sent me messages because their son or daughter has been talking about her and sharing stories of her antics at school. Those who are brave and kind enough to share them do me a great favour. I love hearing stories about Annaliese, particularly of times when we weren't together. Hearing that she used to queue up behind Milo and kiss him on the back of the neck makes me laugh. It sums her up beautifully. She was cheeky, affectionate and didn't care for the rules. '*No kissing at school,*' her class teacher admonished me in the playground at pick up one day. So, if those little tales pop up share them, because they are literally priceless for us.

- Try to get comfortable with sadness. It's part of your friend's reality now and that's okay. Learning to live with sadness is something that *can* be done, but if everyone around you is constantly trying to cheer you up, get you to focus on the positive, and do anything they can to avoid acknowledging what has happened, then it's hard, as the bereaved parent, to believe that your sadness is okay. I've learned to almost embrace those feelings of sadness and devastation. They come over me in waves at unexpected moments and that's okay. I am not ashamed to show my authentic self to others, but I know that's not how everyone feels – my partner, for example, is the complete opposite. Reactions to grief are as individual as your fingerprints and however your friend is responding to their grief, let them know that it's totally okay.

- Practical help is particularly valuable – not just in the early days but also as the months and years tick by. Help can be as simple as a home-cooked meal left on the doorstep, mowing the grass or making phone calls on their behalf. A friend of ours contacted a whole host of bereavement charities to find out what was on offer in terms of support and from that, helped us to know what we had to do next. Practical help can also be more involved, like using your professional experience to navigate a particular situation the bereaved family is facing (legal, medical, mental health and so on). Anything you can do practically, is something that your bereaved friend will genuinely appreciate and treasure.

- Make a note of their child's birthday and anniversary dates and proactively make contact on those dates to let them know you are thinking of them and remembering happy times together. A text or WhatsApp message is quick and easy to send and can mean so much.

- Include their child's name in a Christmas card every year. This is so simple, but so meaningful. A couple of friends still send me a card around Annaliese's birthday which is kind and thoughtful and makes me feel loved and supported.

Occasions

At first, there are SO many triggers around dates, days of the week and even times of the day. I remember that Fridays were hard for me for the first few months thinking, *'this time last week, this time 2 weeks ago etc..'*. Ultimately that sort of thinking is unhelpful, it changes nothing, but somehow you can't escape it. Once you've got past that, you might find the date of the month on which your child died bothers you – I found it tough for a while. However, four years on I can honestly say that I don't think about Fridays or the 25th of every month in that way anymore. There are still plenty of calendar date triggers to trip me up though. I've learnt over the years that for me, the lead up to the big dates is always harder than the actual day itself. Personally, there are probably four dates that really get to me: Annaliese's birthday, the anniversary of her death, the first day of a new school year and Christmas.

I've now learned how to best cope with them and I know that they will come and go. On those days I give myself permission to feel sad, to go 'underground' a little, to ignore social media. The first day back at school - *'stop growing up it's going too fast'* - photos can be challenging to see. I cope by doing exactly what it is that *I* need to do to get by.

Often that means including Annaliese in some way – for example, we still have a cake on her birthday, complete with candles, and we all sing Happy Birthday. I write her a letter every year in the run up to the anniversary of her death, spilling out my thoughts and emotions, talking to her exactly as if she were here. I print them and put them in a folder in her bedroom. At Christmas we still buy both children a new bauble for the tree, a tradition we had before she died. I choose things that I know she would love – a beautiful ceramic Alice in Wonderland figurine, a pink flamingo, whatever it is – because it makes me think of her and when I gaze at the tree, Annaliese is still a part of our Christmas. There's no getting away from the fact that the first Christmas is excruciatingly painful. I felt like I was standing on the edge of a very tall precarious cliff for the entire month of December. I couldn't cope with festive music, did zero socialising, dug my fingernails into the palms of my hand as I attended the school nativity for the sake of my son. I was surrounded by Annaliese's classmates. It was agony, but I did it, I survived and I got through. I'm not saying that's the right approach for everyone, I know many bereaved parents who simply didn't do Christmas thatfirst year or any year since - it's a very individual path to tread. All I know for sure is that you must do what feels right for you and be kind and compassionate to yourself.

We chose to spend that first Christmas at a wonderful close family friends' house rather than be at home. It was a place Annaliese had never been to, so we didn't have any memories of her there to cope with. Being somewhere different eased the pressure just a little. Every Christmas after that we've managed to be at home. It's always an emotional experience but every year it gets a little bit easier and our traditions continue to include Annaliese which feels important to us. I try to avoid things I know are going to be particularly difficult, for example I switch the TV channel over if there's an advert for a girls' toy that I know she would love. I used to absolutely love any programmes that were hospital or medical related, now they are an immediate trigger, and I can't cope with it. I don't look at little girls' clothes in shops and I actively avoid those aisles or areas. I've found it helpful to focus on doing what makes me feel better, rather than focusing on what makes me feel worse. Rest assured though, sometimes I scroll through photos, cling on to her favourite cuddly toy and lay sobbing on her bed. There are times, I've realised, when you've just got to 'give in' to the pain and let it out. There's absolutely no shame in that. In fact, I'd argue it's necessary for survival.

A new school year has always been particularly hard. I've tried to rationalise why I get so anxious, short tempered and emotional around then and have concluded the following:

Firstly, the new school year coincides with my birthday and I hate that Annaliese is not here to make a fuss of me. My son always seems angry and uncaring on that day which I think is because he's cross that he's the only one here and feels extra pressure to make me happy. This (perceived) pressure can thus have a negative effect.

Secondly, I think it's because I know exactly what she should be doing on that day - wearing new school uniform, starting a new class, getting taller and more mature and of course I see all her classmates doing exactly that. It's super hard so I try to get in and out of school as fast as I possibly can that day. Close friends understand and give me the space I need. They accept that I'm not being rude and that I just need time to hide for a bit. This year, Annaliese's class will be finishing primary school and I am already experiencing low level anxiety about that. They are growing up, they are moving on, they are doing exactly what they should be doing, and she's not here to do any of it. It's totally unfair.

What have I learnt?

- It gets easier. Well, it has done for me in any case. It's impossible to believe that for the first couple of years, but I can honestly say that whilst I still hold so much sadness and grief, still break down and sob, still find it almost impossible to believe, and still wish with every cell of my body that Annaliese was here – I am starting to find it less intense, less terrifying, less brutal.

- I have learnt to allow myself the space to feel low. I know these days are coming so I am kind to myself when I need to be. I know, for example, that in the month leading up to the anniversary of Annaliese's death, I feel a crushing pressure in my body which intensifies as we get towards *'the date'*. I make sure I keep my diary as free as I need to, and I don't take on extra responsibilities around that time. I face into it and let it happen because guess what? I can't stop it.

- After a couple of years, I felt like I was starting to see some 'blue sky' and this was how I described it to others. The clouds were gradually breaking a little and that gave me hope - which is what I want to give to you. At first I couldn't believe that I would ever see blue sky again - despite other bereaved parents reassuring me that I would - but I lived through and got to experience it. I kept going, day by day and it's how I've survived this long.

- Experience has taught me that I will get through these dates. I now understand that for me the build up to them is usually worse than the actual day itself.

What can your support crew do to help?

- Remember the important dates. If you know someone whose child has died make a note of this date in your diary FOREVER. I can guarantee you they will want to know you are thinking of them and their child. Send a card, drop them a text, leave a scented candle at their doorstep. Just let them know you remember.
- There are so many ways to show that you care. Some friends sent me a beautiful rose plant called Princess, other friends donate to charity at Christmas because they aren't buying Annaliese a present anymore and as I've mentioned before, close friends have a photo of Annaliese in their house which really touches my heart.
- I remember being totally panicked about how to mark the first anniversary so we decided to start a 'tradition'. We would have a day out to do something nice and try to occupy ourselves and get through it. This was probably more for our then six-year-old

son than us, but it meant we needed to be proactive and think about it. That first year fell on a Saturday and our friend Alex (who had two children aged 8 and 6 at the time), gave up her whole day to accompany us on the anniversary trip. She helped with our son, keeping him occupied so that Matt and I could sit together at the precise moment Annaliese died the year before. Alex then walked around the memorial garden with me looking for the perfect spot to leave a stone I'd painted for Annaliese. Alex was just there every moment of the day. It was extraordinarily selfless and helped us get through it. I know that when she went home she had a big glass of bubbles and a good cry. It's not just us that misses our girl, it's our support crew too.

- As well as anniversaries, birthdays are important too. I've got a lovely friend called Ruth who every year for Annaliese's birthday, used to give me a beautiful candle to burn which was so thoughtful. Knowing people care and remember is immensely powerful.

- Christmas is another big hurdle to face. I felt almost rigid with fear as that first December approached. Everything about it felt like a trigger for me. The music, the TV ads, the relentless cheeriness and excitement. I was emotionally fragile and vulnerable. There were many things my support crew did to help at that time. They acted like minders at the school nativity so we didn't have to make polite chit chat with others and they included Annaliese's name in our Christmas cards. I've said this before but it's such a simple gesture yet is SO important. Some may find this strange and maybe I would have done 'before', however I can honestly say that seeing cards arrive without Annaliese included, feels beyond painful. If you don't know what to say, 'always remembering Annaliese', is a good way to approach it. Even if you think it's weird, just DO IT. Annaliese is still our daughter, she is still a part of our family and we still think of her every minute of every single day. Any cards that I send I sign, *'and always Annaliese x'*, hence the title of this book.

Your Relationship

The pressure that child loss puts on your relationship is intense. Coping and living with a loss as fundamental as this is extraordinarily hard. The person you were before it happened no longer exists, but a new version of yourself does. Bearing in mind that you are both changed and are dealing with your grief and loss differently, it's no surprise that your relationship finds itself in a pressure cooker situation. I can only talk of my personal experiences but from conversations with friends in a similar position, I think a lot of what Matt and I have felt is quite common.

In the first few weeks, we clung to each other like limpets. We were 'lucky' in that we were both with Annaliese in the hospital and so went through that dreadful experience together. It all happened so fast that if only one of us had been there, I think we would have struggled not to blame the other for not intervening, for not saving her. As it was, Matt and I experienced her death minute by minute by each other's side. Those three painful hours were the worst of both our lives whilst we waited to find out what was wrong with her. In the immediacy of her death we were united and supportive, loving, and close, a 'honeymoon' period that lasted a few weeks until after the funeral. Once we had got through Annaliese's funeral we had to face the rest of our lives and our natural instincts went separate ways.

Matt wanted to escape. He wanted to leave our house, our families, friends and our country. He wanted to be as far away from everything as possible – a classic, running away reaction. He started looking at houses for sale in New Zealand (a country we both absolutely love) and would spend hours trawling through real estate websites, emailing himself details of houses he liked the look of. He would try and show me but I wasn't interested.

My immediate reaction was the total opposite. I didn't want anything else to change, I wanted to stay exactly where I was – I didn't have the mental capacity to consider anything else. I firmly believed that what our five-year-old son needed was stability, he needed to be in the same school, the same house, the same bed, and so did I.

That difference in our immediate reactions caused some real fractures in the first six months. Matt couldn't understand why I wanted to stay, and I couldn't understand how he thought leaving would make anything better. I wanted to be close to and near places Annaliese had been, and Matt felt the opposite. It was a tricky time for us both and I was terrified that one day he would tell me he couldn't do this anymore and set off. I felt so out of control with everything. Matt was worried about money, neither of us were working - we were both self-employed and so whilst lucky not to have the pressure of a job to return to, we had no income - and we started living off our savings which we did for several years. Matt kept asking me, '*How are we going to live the rest of our lives like this?*' I couldn't think beyond the next day. We really were in different places mentally and emotionally.

Somehow, we kept going. Matt started swimming every day and I began to indulge my creative side, spending hours and hours sitting at our kitchen table painting stones and colouring. I couldn't listen to music so got into audio books instead, whereas Matt continued to love his music. I went to bed early, Matt stayed up late. You'd be forgiven for thinking we had separate lives, but we didn't – we just needed to do things our own way. There are no rules, you literally have to 'wing it' the best you can.

I cried a lot in that first six months, the skin around my eyes was sore from the tears. After a while though I remember one day realising, 'Wow – I didn't cry today, so I guess that's progress'.

Matt and I are gender typical I think, in that I'm open and emotional and he's not. Understanding that everyone is different and needs their own space and way of coping is key and was crucial for us.

Lower your expectations of each other for a while. In the early days it's literally about surviving and it's hard seeing someone you love in such pain. I think Matt found my crying episodes uncomfortable to witness. He didn't know what to do, he knew he couldn't make it better so he'd say, *'Come on, she wouldn't want you to be upset,'* which made me cross. I would try and save my emotional breakdowns for when Matt was out, to try and protect him somehow. The ice beneath our feet felt dangerously thin at times.

We decided that we would take our son out of school for six weeks following that first Christmas and go on a trip to give ourselves a change of environment. We wanted a different pace, to get some sunshine on our faces and we also didn't want to spend Annaliese's 8th birthday, our first without her, at home. We left a couple of days after Christmas and came back mid-February. During that time, we tried to make some new, happy memories for ourselves. On Annaliese's birthday we spent the day at Sydney Aquarium and it was impossible to understand why she wasn't with us. Our son celebrated his sixth birthday on the beach. I can't deny it felt good to be somewhere else for a while, but the reality was that all of us were hurting and struggling to make sense of life - it didn't matter if we were in our local neighbourhood or on the other side of the world. There were some wonderful moments, but there were also some horrific ones. After a particularly bad meltdown from our son, when my very easy-going and patient other half just lost it, I remember sitting in the dark in the one room we were all sharing. Our son was asleep, Matt was listening to music on his headphones and I was silently crying in the bathroom. I wanted to fix it all, I wanted to help my lovely boys feel okay again, but I couldn't. It was a really frightening moment. To get me through, all I could do was hope that the next day would be a little easier - and it was.

Matt and I both had therapy during that first year (more of that in another chapter), though I'm not sure how helpful it truly was. It's only been recently, now that we're undergoing therapy as a couple, that it feels as if we are starting to make some progress. Our counsellor is an amazing woman who understands grief, loss, trauma, and adoption, which has made a huge difference. We are beginning to understand ourselves better as individuals, we're exploring the dynamics of our relationship and are getting to grips with the support and understanding that our son needs. You have to put the work in to get somewhere and it took us over three years to be ready for it. We've still got a long way to go - the truth is that each one of us has changed – and we are still struggling to live with the aftershocks of the tsunami which hit when we were least expecting it.

I'm enormously proud of Matt and I for still being together against the odds. We have found a way to live which for the moment is okay. We still make each other laugh, we respect each other and there's a lot of love (though some days more than others).

I think we are both in awe of the other for different reasons and I'd like to take this opportunity to let Matt know he's a great Dad, he's patient, he's kind, and he's fun. He's also a caring, loyal, thoughtful and easy-going partner. I'm so sorry our lives have turned out the way they have and I know we both feel hard done by at times which I believe we have every right to. I'm also sorry to Matt that I don't want to move to Thailand tomorrow (he's still looking at properties all over the world), but who knows? Maybe one day.

What have I learnt?

There's so much, but I guess it boils down to acceptance and understanding. Acceptance that we are different people and need to cope in our own unique ways. There's no right or wrong. There should be no judgement. It's about taking the time to understand what your partner needs from you when they are crashing. There have been times, and still are, when one of us hasn't been able to cope with something – often in relation to parenting our son - and the other seems to find the strength to step in and take the lead. I know Matt has got my back. He's encouraged me in all of the things I've tried since Annaliese died - selling my painted stones, painting watercolours for The Compassionate Friends Christmas cards every year, getting back into a bit of communications consulting, setting up a new business, writing this book... I've had to learn to let Matt be himself and do what he needs. I may not agree, but I understand that it's not my place to judge. We each walk our own paths which are still alongside each other, and I hope we do for many years to come.

What can your support crew do to help?

Relationships are, by their very nature, unique and personal and there's not as much your support crew can do in this area, but here are some things that have helped us:

- Be there to listen. There's no need to offer advice necessarily, but just having a space to get stuff off your chest is helpful.
- If there are surviving children, offer to have them on playdates, take them out for the day – find opportunities to give your friends some time to themselves. We've recently started having a monthly 'date night' where we try not to chat about our loss or our parenting challenges, instead we aim to have a bit of a laugh. For a couple of hours we will suspend reality and it's time now that I really look forward to. It reminds me why Matt and I love each other and why we are such good friends. Having someone to babysit and force us to have that night is a practical thing you can do to help your friend or relative.

- Keep inviting your friends to things. For a long time we turned down all invitations, but gradually we began to accept a few. It's easy to stop asking people when they always say no, but I really appreciated the friends who continued to include me, no matter how many times I declined. We're now at a stage where we can go out with a small group of friends and enjoy ourselves. Big parties are still off limits for now, but we've made progress. So, keep the invitations coming and please don't be offended if your friend or family member doesn't attend. They may do, one day.

Surviving Siblings

If I've cried a thousand tears over losing Annaliese, I've cried just as many about the loss and trauma our son must learn to live with. My heart breaks for him almost daily. I know how hard it is as an adult trying to make sense of what has happened – so imagining what it feels like for a 5-year-old (now 10-year-old) is impossible.

His (and our) story is further complicated by the fact that both he and Annaliese were adopted. If you know anything about adoption you will know that adopted children carry within themselves a level of trauma already. They have been removed from their birth family, moved to a foster family (sometimes more than one) and then finally to their adoptive family. When you add this trauma to the sudden overnight loss of a sibling, it's very easy to see why our son has found life and his emotions difficult to navigate over the past few years.

Grief is complex and the fact our children are adopted adds a layer of additional complication that is hard to explain unless you are living it. It's become clearer to us as the months have ticked by that sibling survivor guilt is a very real thing. There have been times where I've felt we've been punished twice over – losing Annaliese and parenting a child traumatised by the sudden death of his big sister. The truth is that he's scared and unsure about the world now. One day she was here, the next she wasn't. She left him, and his parents are different now too.

The challenge is that his fear and anxiety manifest themselves in anger, aggression and at times, physical violence. Learning to look beyond the behaviour to the feeling, and then beyond the feeling to the need, is something we had no idea about before. It's easy to judge our son and our parenting based on what you see - there have been plenty of times I wished he could wear a t-shirt which said, *'My 7-year-old sister died really suddenly and I'm struggling to cope with it'*. I think people would be less judgemental and more understanding if they knew what he was dealing with. Most of the time he manages to 'mask', which means he hides how he's really feeling about a situation. He copes fairly well in school, but when he comes home and can really relax and be himself, it can be pretty tough on all of us.

When it came to bedtime of the day we told him he asked if he could sleep in her bed and wear her pyjamas. We said of course. It broke my heart. I had to put him to bed, stroke his forehead and sing him a lullaby just as I had done to Annaliese a couple of nights before. I literally collapsed into a heap the moment I left the room.

He wanted to wear Annaliese's dressing gown and sometimes he squeezed his (too big) feet into her little pink bunny slippers or took one of her cuddly toys to bed. It was obviously a way for him to feel close to her. Generally he doesn't like other people bringing up Annaliese, but he's happy to talk about her when he feels like it. I've noticed he says 'my sister' rather than saying her name. I'm not sure why – is it because it feels more like she belongs to him when he says that? There have been so many things he's said to me over the years that literally make me want to sob and just hold him close, but it's important that he feels comfortable talking to us about Annaliese, about his feelings and about death – so we try our absolute best to be strong. Seeing us cry is part of helping him to understand his feelings, but seeing us cry all the time isn't helpful.

As with everything in life, it's about balance. We are careful to talk about her in a positive light as well as remembering all the mischief she got up to. She wasn't perfect and we want him to know that. He has many photos of them both together in his bedroom that he asked for, and some of her cuddly toys in his bed. Last year his class had a lesson about loss and grief. We had discussed it with his teacher beforehand and I spoke to him about it – giving him the option to skip the class as I worried it might be too painful. He said that he wanted to be there, so I told him how brave he was. We did have an exit plan arranged with the teacher though, just in case. I then reminded him that he might be able to help some of his friends understand what grief and loss feel like but that it was okay if he couldn't cope. Sure enough, he lasted only a few minutes before becoming emotionally distressed and was taken off to do something else - but at least he wanted to try. Poor kid, it's a lot to deal with.

We continue to celebrate Annaliese's birthday and her adoption anniversary (both with chocolate cake, which is his choice), and on the anniversary of her death we talk about Annaliese and try to do something nice as a family to distract ourselves from the sadness. I remember on the first anniversary he said to us, 'We're doing really well aren't we Mum?' I asked him what he meant. 'I mean we are doing really well trying to have a happy life without her'. Christ it's hard.

This year on the fourth anniversary, as I lay in his bed for a cuddle at the end of the day, I talked to him about all the lovely messages I'd been sent. 'What, they remember the date?' he asked, sounding surprised. I told him that lots of people miss her and think about us, which I think made him feel loved and cared for.

Our son feels so alone, he told us that a lot at the beginning, so just after the first anniversary we got a dog. A gorgeous Labradoodle puppy that we called Gus Gus after Annaliese's favourite character in Cinderella – the greedy little mouse. Another way we are still including her in our lives. It was a complete surprise for our son. He came home from school to find this little bundle of dark brown fluff in our living room.

'I've always wanted to be a big brother,' he said and 'I'm not alone anymore'. Then he went upstairs to get a framed photo of him and his sister to put on top of the dog crate, 'So that Gus Gus can meet Annaliese'. All these little comments are part of his healing, part of him learning how to live without her though I wish he didn't have to. It feels so unfair – his life is changed forever. He's the boy at school whose big sister died (they were at the same school), he's the one on his own without a sibling every weekend, on Christmas morning, on family holidays – it's bloody unfair and I hate it. He deserves more. She deserved more.

He started having weekly play therapy about four months after she died in 2018. The lockdowns in 2020 meant that wasn't possible so he had a break for a while. We then found a new therapist who, after 18 months working with him, seems to be making some progress. It's taking our son a long time to feel safe enough to access his feelings and understandably he just wants to lock them away and hide from reality. Despite all of these challenges, I want him to know that he's an amazing boy and I'm very proud to be his Mum. He's coping with so much, yet he's keeping up at school, has friends, is an absolute superstar at the skate park and, like us, just keeps going. My darling boy, I want you to know (presuming you will read this one day) that trying to make you happy, confident and the best version ofyourself is my life's purpose now. Your sister would be so proud of you, never forget that.

When things are tough and he's cross and angry, it's hard not to feel rejected and despondent. We feel guilty all the time and I worry that at some level he blames us for 'letting' her die. I always used to say to the kids that it was our job as parents to keep them safe – he must wonder why we didn't do that for Annaliese that day. I punish myself by wondering it too at times.

His fear is almost palpable. Yesterday whilst we were driving, he said to me 'Mum, do you know everything is dangerous'. He went on, 'the trees, walking, driving…' He's hardwired now to see potential danger at every turn which is so sad for a young boy. He has an inherent distrust and fear about doctors and hospitals too. During the pandemic in the UK at 8pm on a Thursday night we used to clap for the NHS outside our doors and through our open windows. I did it with him that first week and afterwards he asked me, 'Why did we do that Mum when they didn't save my sister?'

We didn't do it again.

What have I learnt?

- That coping with and caring for a surviving sibling is very hard at times. I'm learning (and it's taken some time to get to this point) to understand what lies behind his behaviour and not to take the things he says and does personally.
- That parenting an adopted child with this additional layer of trauma is really tricky. You need the patience of a saint and the skin of a rhino (I have neither).
- That being on the same page as my partner as far as our parenting strategies are concerned is critical for the health of our relationship. In truth, most of the arguments we have centre around this point. We've found that doing DDP therapy (Dyadic Development Practice) has really helped us progress in this area, as well as embracing therapeutic parenting as a strategy (well, embracing might be stretching the truth a little but we are doing our best). DDP was created by clinical psychologist Dan Hughes as a treatment for families with adopted or fostered children who

had experienced neglect and abuse in their birth families and suffered from significant developmental trauma. It's based on and brings together attachment theory, what we understand about developmental trauma, the neurobiology of trauma, caregiving, intersubjectivity theory and child development. It's hard work and is counter intuitive at times, but it IS beginning to help our son feel safer, supported, and loved.

- Shouting at him, punishing him, and shaming him for his behaviours which at times are intense, achieves nothing. Kindness, understanding, and love are the way forward – every single time. That doesn't mean that I don't shout – I'm human, I do but it's never helpful and often escalates the situation.

- We have found that days out as a family frequently end in massive emotional meltdowns. So, we tend to take one day each at the weekend to do something with him (90% of the time that's going to a skatepark) whilst the other one gets some time alone. It works for us at the moment.

- I've learnt that a combination of being adopted and being bereaved makes his life very hard. When Annaliese died, I couldn't ever have foreseen that supporting and caring for our son would take so much of my time and energy.

What can your support crew do to help?

- If you are a friend or family member with a child or children, sensitively help them to understand what has happened and that the bereaved sibling (their friend) will be feeling very sad and may start to act a little differently because of it. I remember a classmate saying to our son at football club before school, 'I know your sister's dead.' This was within a few days of it happening. Luckily (a) I was there to hear it and be there for him and (b) the moment passed, and the kids just got on with playing. The boys were only five and so I totally understand why he said it (it was factually correct), but anything you as parents can do to help your children react with sensitivity would be helpful.

- Suspend judgement. It's likely you have no idea what it's like to cope with this level of grief and loss. There have been plenty of times when my son's behaviour has been (and continues to be) what I would previously have considered unacceptable. He can be very disrespectful to us - 'shut up you idiot', 'shut your yap' and 'why should I care?' are a few of his favourites. He gets physical with us; he's easily frustrated and sometimes aggressive. He has a very heightened sense of unfairness; he feels like the world is against him and finds it really hard when things don't go his way. This can cause awkward situations with other children and parents. I'm sure there have been times when people looked at him and us and thought we were not nice individuals and questioned whether they wanted their kids to play with him. I can tell you now that all three of us have felt shame about that. At times we are a pressure cooker of emotions that are easily upset – we need people to be patient with us. Please try and explain to your kids that it's very hard for families who have lost a child. Please persevere, invite them for playdates - our son loves going to other people's houses, partly because I think he feels very lonely on his own now. Invite them to parties, offer to take them to the park. It means SO much to me that there are a few friends who have been capable of accepting our son (and us) for who we are now. I have been grateful to them many times over. To know he is accepted exactly as he is, for now, is a precious gift.

- There are some amazing resources out there to support children with their grief – as a friend you could buy some books to help with conversations around death and grief – just buy them, give them to your friend or family member and let them make the decision on whether it's helpful or not. It might not be right for now, but in a few months' time it could be invaluable in helping a conversation happen between parent and child. At the back of this book, you will find a list of children's reading material that my son has on his bookshelf which you might find helpful.

School

If your child was still at school when they died, then the way the school reacts can make a big impact - for better or worse. Annaliese was in Year 2 of primary school when she died, and her little brother was in Reception. There are many siblings between these classes and so it had a dramatic impact on the school which only has seven classes in total. I think we were exceptionally lucky that the Head was someone who already had a great connection with our daughter. I know she was personally devastated by what happened and her support was extraordinary at the time and in the years that followed. So, here's what the school did that made a difference to us:

- The Head and Deputy Head visited us at home a few days after Annaliese died which was during half term. Firstly, they wanted to share their condolences, but they also brought with them everything they could lay their hands on connected to Annaliese from her time at school. Her workbooks, her favourite cuddly cat (which I later found out from her classmates she called Mrs Fluffyboots!) and there was a big box filled with copies of her latest school photo. Anything connected to her was and remains so precious to us - I really appreciated them bringing those parts of Annaliese's life over as soon as they were able. I remember the Head also gave us a big pillar candle that sat on our kitchen table smelling gorgeous for months. A small but powerful gesture.

- They listened. Really listened to how we wanted to approach things and respected our wishes almost to the letter. We were able to agree exactly what was written to all parents and proofread the letter before it went out. Public Health England were involved because of the infection Annaliese caught, so other parents had to be given advice on what symptoms to look for. Despite others asking if they could, we didn't want flowers laid around the school. Our son was in Reception and we thought it would be too much for him (and probably us) to cope with seeing a shrine every day.

The school literally took our lead at every step and it made such a difference during those first dark days.

- Annaliese's class teacher worked with Year 2 to put together the most amazing scrapbook of memories. Each child had a page and shared something they remembered about their times with Annaliese. It is full of photos and drawings and bundles of love. It is very special indeed and I look at it every now and then – it makes me cry and laugh in equal measure. Some of the stories they share are hysterical and bring our beautiful daughter to life in a way that only another seven-year-old could.

- The extra care and attention the school gave our son (and continue to) was absolutely wonderful. The Head kept a close eye on him and told him that if ever he wanted to talk to her about his sister (or anything else) then he just needed to come to her office. I'd given her a framed photo of Annaliese which she kept on her desk until she retired, and she told our son that if ever he wanted to come and look at the photo, he could. There were times when he went into that office and chatted to her – I know he felt safe and for that I'm eternally thankful.

When we talked to them about the idea of taking our son out of school and travelling for a few weeks they gave us their blessing and told us they would manage the associated paperwork.

- In the first couple of years, the school reserved seats for us at the front of assemblies, nativities etc. so that we didn't have to queue with hordes of other parents and could arrive last minute and sit down, eyes forward, gritting our teeth. I don't think I would have been able to attend otherwise. I just felt too vulnerable and self-conscious. The school supported our wish for another set of rollover bars to be installed in the playground in Annaliese's memory. She absolutely loved the rollover bars and was infamous for sneaking off when she should have been lining up to go into class for one last cheeky go! They are there today – painted pink with a small gold butterfly plaque which reads 'Remembering Annaliese and her love of the rollover bars. We miss your cheeky smile and your warm hugs'. I hear they are much enjoyed by others which she would love.

- As our children are both adopted, the Head took a holistic approach to the pupil premium fund she had for school on their behalf. We used some of that money to support therapy for all three of us during those early months. She knew that as a family we needed the extra support and she never made us feel uncomfortable about it.

- Around the first anniversary, the Head led a special lesson with Annaliese's classmates to talk about Annaliese and share their memories of her. This continued each year until the pandemic.I used to loan her the memory scrapbook and Mrs Fluffyboots (cuddly toy) for the occasion and she would share with me how the lesson had gone. It made me sob of course - those kids had lost their friend, literally just like that. It must have been very hard for all of them to understand.

- For the fourth anniversary this year, her Year 6 class had a session with their wonderful Reception teacher during which they recalled experiences from their first year at school as innocent five-year-olds. They talked about how they remembered Annaliese falling asleep during carpet time and cutting her hair in secret under the table. They each wrote memories which were sent home for us. To have her celebrated and honoured in that way means so much. All of this was organised with our consent and input and the school have been so incredibly respectful.

- Instead of joining a full hall of people for parents evening chats we were given private appointments which helped us enormously. We felt very self-conscious in those early years.

What have I learnt?

- That people want to help, to support and try to do whatever they can to alleviate just a little of your pain and disorientation.

- That a feeling of self-consciousness is very prevalent within a small community like a primary school. There's no real way to avoid it, so you just have to get on with it.

- That an understanding of the life your child had at school and how others saw them is absolutely precious. We received cards from people we didn't know but whose children knew Annaliese. They shared little stories with us that warmed our breaking hearts and forced a smile onto our faces.

What can your support crew do to help?

All parents at the school naturally felt shocked and very sorry for us. The pity was quite hard to cope with, it still is sometimes. But there's no real way around that I don't think, their reactions were understandable and so were ours. Things our close friends did to help included:

- In the first few days back at school a week after Annaliese died, our friends literally waited for us on the pavement where we parked our car (ensuring there was a space) and walked with us the 500 yards to the playground. It felt a bit like a scene from *Reservoir Dogs* as we were 'protected' on all sides, front and back. We weren't ready to face any conversations of condolence, it was all I could do to be upright and walking in those early days. We would leave after dropping our son off and I'd sob on the way back to the car. The world looked the same, though it was anything but, for us.

- Inviting our son for playdates when he was lonely and sad about life – and being understanding that his behaviour was unpredictable (and at times, still is).

- Sitting either side of us at school assemblies/performances – again 'protecting' us from having to chat to people, which at the time felt impossible. Small talk was agony for a while, but we're able to cope with that again now.

- Annaliese was included in her school years leavers' hoodie jumper which was very meaningful to me – to know that she is still thought of, still in some way a part of that class. When I was given her hoodie I felt overwhelmingly sad. I wanted to see her wearing it, but I'm so thankful she's been included. I want her to count. She was here. She is loved. She matters. The hoodie sits on the back of my office chair and if I'm feeling low I wrap it around myself and let myself feel surrounded by her.

Professional Support

There is absolutely no doubt that the professional support we have had and continue to have has helped us, however, it's not necessarily an easy journey to get to the point we're at now – feeling that we have the right people in place. Depending on your personality you may feel drawn towards therapy or not. I'm a talker and have always found sharing my thoughts and emotions easy; Matt is the complete opposite. For him, the idea of having to sit in a room with a stranger and talk to them about the most painful experience of his life was like pouring a ton of salt onto an open wound. A close friend persuaded him to see someone that she recommended in those first few weeks and I think he was too weak to protest. In hindsight, I'm not sure they were the right person for him BUT, at that moment, it was just important that he had somewhere to go, someone to speak to that wasn't me or anyone who knew him previously. I also rushed into the arms of a counsellor who was recommended to me in the early weeks, but I soon realised they weren't right for me or what I needed at that time. After a few sessions of sitting there sobbing and them telling me how sad and awful it all was, I decided to take a break. I was lucky to have friends I could sob to and the counselling wasn't really helping me.

However, a few months later, following a diagnosis of PTSD (post-traumatic stress disorder), I started to look for a more focused therapist, one that specialised in EMDR (eye movement desensitisation and reprocessing). I hoped that we could, together, get to the heart of some of my most acute triggers. At this stage the inquest was looming and I wanted to have some techniques to help me cope with facing it. This style of therapy felt much more useful to me. There were still lots of tears obviously, but it was a more structured approach and I felt I made some progress during those initial few months. I then took a break of almost two years, during which time many people tried to encourage me to get some support, but I knew I just wasn't in the right headspace. I was busy coping with our son's grief and the subsequent behaviours that were getting more and more intense, and simply just putting one foot in front of the other. I knew that I would get back to therapy when it felt right.

Not surprisingly in 2020 the pandemic and subsequent UK lockdowns were the straws that broke the camel's back. Being locked up together 24/7 was extremely hard, particularly on our then seven-year-old son. He'd been seeing a play therapist for over a year but I wasn't convinced they were the right person for him, and they didn't really demonstrate a collaborative relationship which was what I felt we needed.

Things seemed like they were falling apart and I was crying almost daily again, so I reached out once more for professional support. I feel very fortunate that two separate friends recommended therapists based on their own personal experiences: one for our son and one for us as a couple/family. It took quite a few months to get going as there was a lot of paperwork and phone calls to begin with. We also needed to get funding agreed through the Adoption Support Fund and were extremely lucky that a subsidy was available for us. We had been living predominantly on savings for 3 years and spending hundreds of pounds on therapy would have stressed us out.

We are 18 months into working with both professionals and I believe it's starting to make a difference. They demonstrate a collaborative relationship, are extremely considerate of our complicated situation, and understand and have experience of adoption and trauma which has been essential for our therapy. We have regular review calls together to look holistically at us as a family which is the only way to make real progress in my experience.

Matt and I are learning a new way of parenting (Therapeutic Parenting) which has been a challenge for us but is starting to work. Our son is coping with so much trauma, from his adoption and then the sudden death of his big sister and then into lockdown - understanding the impact of that on himand the resulting behaviours is the only way we can move forwards. Of course, parenting is hard at the best of times, so at the worst of times when you feel like you are drowning in sadness, it can feel bloody impossible. But Matt and I are determined to do our best and when we don't get it right we take time to review what happened, talk about how we might do it differently and learn from whatever meltdown has occurred. It's exhausting but it's our job as parents. I don't really expect others to get it – but just need acceptance of how I am coping with it on any given day. Don't be judgemental or tell me how you think I should be 'by now'. I am going to grieve forever. It's never going to be okay that my daughter died aged seven without warning. Never. It doesn't mean that I'm not going to feel happiness about other things, it doesn't mean that I'm stuck in the past, it doesn't mean that I'm wallowing in sorrow. It just means that I miss her and I'm living with a huge amount of sadness. It runs through my body just as my blood runs through my veins. It just is. I can't stop it; I don't want to stop it. Living alongside my grief is what I am learning to do. Don't judge, don't try to 'fix' me, just accept me for who I am now and try to understand what I need.And for my part I hope you never get to truly understand what this feels like.

For us as a couple it's been useful to have the time and space to look back to our own childhoods and to understand what informs us as parents ourselves. We've had to be open, honest and embrace the vulnerability that therapy of this nature brings. It comes naturally for me, but for Matt it's been a big ask. His willingness to try shows genuine bravery though when truth be told he'd rather not. I hope the professionals we have found will be in our lives for a good while to come. I've come to trust them, respect them, listen to them, and learn from them. They are managing to move us slowly forwards, inch by inch, to a place where we can accept and cope with our tremendous loss and learn to live with our new reality.

What have I learnt?

- Help is out there but finding the right person for you may take time. Don't give up if the first therapist you talk to doesn't feel right or 'make you better'.
- I've also come to understand that you need to be ready to really open the wounds and dig deep into the pain to start to heal. It took me almost three years to get to that place, it can take much longer. Be patient and listen to what feels right for you.
- I'd also recommend talking to your GP if you feel you need some additional support. Whilst it's not always the answer, medication used responsibly has enabled both of us to cope better at times when we experienced depressive feelings and overwhelm. I think the stigma around mental health is definitely improving, but we both felt reticent to seek the help we understandably needed.
- Progress is slow, painfully slow at times, but even a tiny bit of progress is worth grabbing with both hands. For me progress has

come in the shape of being able to cope with painful occasions better - I've just had my first Christmas Day without tears in four years. I can also attend school events without being paralysed by fear and paranoia (we recently attended a parents' quiz night and it was brilliant fun) and am able to talk about Annaliese with genuine love, fondness and humour (not all of the time obviously, but some of the time at least). I've also learned how to approach parenting our son differently. I've learned to understand his trauma better and support him accordingly.

What can your support crew do to help?

- If you have any experience of therapists that you really rate, share their details or offer to put them in touch. Navigating a sea of therapists is really daunting and hard, so personal recommendations are very valuable.

- Think about some of the practicalities that you could help with if your family member or friend is having professional support. Do they need a babysitter for their other child(ren)? Could you host a playdate? Could you take or pick up their kids from school? Give them a lift to an appointment if they don't drive? – that kind of thing.

- Be encouraging but don't be overly pushy. During the two-year gap I had between therapists many people told me that I should be getting support and seeing someone, but I knew I wasn't ready. Respecting the individuals' instincts is helpful - or it was for me.

- If you are truly worried about the mental health and safety of your friend, then you might need to be a little more proactive. At the back of this book are a list of organisations which could be helpful to contact.

- Depending on the circumstances it could be helpful to try and identify professional support routes that come with financial assistance.

Finding Your Tribe

This wouldn't have occurred to me before, but it makes complete sense. No one can get what it's like to lose a child unless they have lost one too. I've got some incredible friends who have walked beside me since that fateful day, but even they can't truly 'get' how I feel. That's where finding your tribe comes in. Within days of Annaliese dying, a lovely friend of ours, who had been researching where we could go for help, gave me a list of places with contact numbers and the type of support available.

With this list I started to make phone calls, one of which was to *The Compassionate Friends*, a charity set up in 1969 purely to support bereaved parents, grandparents, and siblings. I'd never heard of them before – why would I? I spoke to a lovely kind volunteer and calmly said my daughter had died and I was wondering what resources or support might be available for us. I clearly recall her asking when

Annaliese had died and my reply, 'Last week'.

Her reaction confused me a little, she seemed to almost draw breath before responding. 'I'm so very sorry,' she said, 'it's such early days for you'. I didn't really get her reaction at the time, though now of course it's bloody obvious. I was still in shock although I didn't know it and was just going through the motions of being practical and asking for help. It gave me something to do.

A few days after that first phone call (when a package of leaflets was dispatched to me), I got a call from our local group leader. Sue listened as I told her what had happened, and she shared with me that she'd lost a precious son Joe when he was twelve. Sue was several years ahead of me on the journey, and she was the first bereaved parent I'd spoken to since Annaliese died. I knew that she understood exactly how I was feeling. She was warm, kind, empathetic and told me that whilst it would take a long time, I would be okay. It gave me a glimmer of hope – the tiniest glimmer, but that felt so comforting.

It became clear in the coming months (and years) that this group of people would become very important and dear to me. Although I've only met a handful of them in the flesh, the connections between us run very deep. They are my tribe. As the name implies, the compassion overflows – we talk about our children (for me mostly on Facebook but there are face-to-face meet ups too) and we talk without any fear of judgement or making each other uncomfortable. All our circumstances are different, but the unconditional support and love has been something I've come to really value.

These are people just like me whose life has been turned upside down by something they never expected to have to cope with. I've come to know their children through the photos and stories we share – Sophie, Evie, Adam, Megan, Ollie, Isaac, Leon, Skye, Simon, Rachael, Jasper, Bissie, Lily, Rosie, Joe, Libby, Dylan, Max – I could go on writing names for the rest of this book. They have come to know Annaliese too and I truly love having a place that I can celebrate her, tell stories and show off some of the wonderful photos I have. I also do this on my personal Facebook page – but the level of honesty (and sometimes pain) that I can express to my Compassionate Friends is on another level.

We support each other as a group. When someone is really struggling we are there to listen, to send out love and to say we understand.

When someone has something positive to tell (like being able to face decorating the Christmas tree), we share those small steps of progress. I've learnt a lot from this group, and I've been privileged to be able to give something back – whether it's raising money for The Compassionate Friends ahead of my 50th birthday (a few months after Annaliese died) or providing watercolour paintings for the charity Christmas Cards every year. I also try to offer hope to others joining our group more recently than me. It helped me so much. I couldn't imagine that the pain wouldn't always cut so deep. I felt I would never survive and now I feel compelled to support others, as I was supported, if I can.

When I made that first phone call I had absolutely no idea how much I would come to rely on The Compassionate Friends family for support, love, understanding, acceptance, and encouragement. Now I can't imagine my life without them.

What have I learnt?

- For me, finding a group of people who truly understand has been enormously comforting. There's no denying that we are a group whose lives are edged with the most profound grief imaginable, but we can hold each other's pain, listen without judgement and prop each other up when needed. Some are coming to terms with losing their only precious child, some are facing inquests, some are coping with the pain of suicide. Whatever the circumstances, there's comfort in being with people that get it.
- I very quickly wanted to become an active member of this group – I'm naturally communicative and find sharing my feelings very helpful. Matt felt differently. He did join the dads Facebook group but is a passive rather than active member – we are two opposites on the spectrum in that respect.
- I have almost immersed myself in the understanding of grief. I read many books and blogs on the subject, watch TED talks, listen to podcasts – for me knowledge is power, it helps me cope

and is part of the motivation for writing this book. Matt would rather not focus on his grief in that way.

- Acceptance that everyone grieves differently is another important part of the bereavement jigsaw puzzle. I've learnt that I'm not alone, far from it. Whilst my heart aches for every new parent who joins The Compassionate Friends, it has helped me get nearer to acceptance and to understanding that terrible things happen to children every single day of the year. It wasn't anything I did wrong; we were just terribly unlucky. Seeing my fellow bereaved parents opening their hearts, carrying on their life with dignity and compassion has been truly inspiring and helped me to keep going. We – you - are true warriors and I stand shoulder to shoulder with you all.

What can your support crew do to help?

- Understanding that no matter how amazingly supportive you are to your friends, unless you have lost a child too you won't be able to 'get it' in the same way as someone who has. This doesn't diminish the role you can play one little bit, but it's just to be aware they might need more. For me, connecting with other bereaved parents has been so powerful. Their ability to hold my grief, understand my anger and recognise the difficulties in everyday life has made a real difference to me over the years.

- Some people might think that 'surrounding' yourself with other bereaved parents is only going to keep you 'stuck' in a place of deep grief, make you focus on the negative rather than trying to look for the positive. The truth is everyone is different. Some people genuinely don't feel they need or want to be part of this group, but for me personally, it's helped me feel less isolated, given me hope, allowed me to be honest and open and also given me the chance to help others and raise money to support The Compassionate Friends.

It might not be something you think you'd want or need but allowing your friend to cope with their grief in a way that feels right for them is the best gift you can give.

Being Kind to Yourself

It's hard to put yourself first when you are literally on your knees with grief and are exhausted both physically and emotionally – but it's critical to find a way to be kind to yourself. You need to look after yourself and recognise that it's okay not to be okay. There are certainly things I have done (and sometimes still do) that aren't conducive to me coping well, so I've listed a few things I've discovered that might help you out too:

- Social media can be hard to handle – particularly during the early weeks and around triggering occasions. I have breaks from it when I need to 'avoid' the rest of the world's happiness. The first time I did this was during the school summer holidays, six weeks after Annaliese died. Seeing photos of happy families out and about wasn't what I needed at that point. I also avoided

Christmas time and I plan to avoid the week that school finishes this year when her class will be leaving primary school. I know that seeing comments like, *'You're growing up too quickly, please stop,'* will make me feel frustrated and resentful, and it's just best that I don't put myself in that position. The people writing and saying those things are my friends and they shouldn't have to censor themselves because of our situation.

- Resting your mind and body (including sleep) is vitally important because you are going to feel exhausted - physically and emotionally for a very long time. In the early weeks you are likely to find sleep evasive, I certainly did, so I took sleeping tablets for a couple of weeks to help me function. I didn't want to stay on them long term (personal choice) so I made a few changes to my sleep routine. I've always been someone that liked an early night (around 10pm, sometimes earlier) as I'm not a good sleeper anyway. To get six hours sleep, I probably need to be in bed for eight hours, so I've made sure I give myself that chance. I also use a pillow mist spray every night to help me relax and I play some calming music specifically designed to help you sleep. The sound of ocean waves is relaxing too. I find it's just enough to distract my brain which will otherwise go into overdrive. I have also become someone who takes the occasional nap in the daytime, either on the sofa, in the garden if it's sunny (I absolutely love the feeling of sunshine on my face) or in bed, and I try hard not to feel guilty about it. A 30-minute switch off is sometimes very helpful.

- Finding an interest. For me it's been doing something creative (painting, drawing, crafting), reading and listening to podcasts. For Matt it's been swimming which he tries to do most days and walking our dog. I have found that 'distracting' my brain has been immensely helpful. Staring into space and going over and over our tragedy didn't get me far. There ARE times when I need to do this, but I recognised that it wasn't helpful to do this all the time. For the first year I found listening to music too hard, I couldn't concentrate on reading and I cried every time I looked at photos or videos. I can do all those things today, which at one point I thought would be an impossibility. My way of coping is to fill my time with being busy. I need a project, an audio book, a cupboard to clear out, a mini-series that I feel addicted to – all these things give me a sense of purpose and that's where writing this book came from. I'm not saying it's right for everyone - listen to your body and mind and do what is right for you. As I said earlier, be kind to yourself and try not to focus on things that you know are going to make you unravel.

- You are coping with possibly the hardest thing life can throw at you, so take it one step at a time. An old friend from university said to me very early on that getting through this was going to be like running a marathon - and at that point I didn't even have my trainers on! I think he was right and that analogy has stuck with me. Step by step I'm running my marathon, one foot in front of the other. I reckon I'm about mile eight or nine now.

What have I learnt?

Lowering my expectations has helped me enormously over the years. Expectations of people, of situations and of life in general. I am aware that this may sound defeatist but honestly, I've found it very liberating and positive. I've learned that if I expect less, I am disappointed less. Acceptance is of course the ultimate destination, but I feel I am someway off that. Acceptance of what's happened is the holy grail and that extends to accepting how people react, behave, and of who you are now and how you choose to live.

What can your support crew do to help?

- It's amazing how random acts of kindness can make someone feel good – a bunch of brightly coloured tulips or daffodils on the doorstep, freshly baked biscuits, a lovely scented candle, passing on a book you've enjoyed, a thoughtful text message, arranging a gentle walk together, getting together over a glass of wine or cup of tea.

- Don't be offended if the person who is bereaved doesn't want to see you, chat in the street or on the doorstep. I have always considered myself an outgoing and sociable person but losing my daughter had a massive impact on my confidence and ability to face people – even good friends. It was as if everything I knew about the world became unhinged and floated around in a way that didn't make sense. Worse, it actually frightened me. I'm gradually finding myself again but I still have periods of time when I 'go to ground' and actively avoid people. It's nothing you've done, it's not about you, it's about how I feel and what I need to do to cope. Allowing your bereaved friend or family member space is so appreciated in my experience. You can drop them a message to say you are thinking of them, that you are there if they need, but then understand that you might not get a reply. Sometimes, connecting with the outside world feels too hard. As the support network my advice would be to not stop asking, even after many 'no' replies - one day they might just be ready to say yes.

Guilt

The guilt is something I am still struggling with. As a parent it's your job to protect your child, to keep them safe from harm. When they die, you have clearly failed at your job. That's absolute rubbish of course, but it's how I still feel. There have been many times when I've poured endlessly over the details of it all – that 'sliding doors' moment when I could have made a different decision which could have made the difference between life and death for my little, innocent girl. Obviously, all circumstances are different, but at some level I think we all blame ourselves at various stages of our grieving journey. Personally, I am furious with myself for not challenging the doctors when they sent us home from hospital the night before she died. Why didn't I insist that they admit her? She walked in unaided but a few short hours later had to leave in a wheelchair due to her leg pain - why didn't I realise that wasn't right, that she couldn't possibly go home? Why did I believe what the doctors told me? When you aren't emotionally invested, it's clear why you believe them – because they are the professionals, and you are not.

As her mother though, I've tortured myself with the 'what ifs' and I know many other bereaved parents do the same. It's hard to live with the knowledge that it could have been so different. But live with the guilt you must.

I've found myself wrestling over other aspects of her life too. Like many adopted children, Annaliese could be challenging to parent; she was hugely anxious and the most defiant child I had ever known. Learning to parent her in the way she needed took us some time. In fact, we were only really getting to grips with what she needed in terms of professional support and parenting in the last nine months of her life. I feel so bad about the times I shouted at her with frustration (like every parent I've ever met does), and the times she sobbed because she was so stressed. I have a particularly vivid image in my mind of her curled up on the floor under my desk, crying loudly because of something or other, and me being cross with her for whatever it was. I hate the memory of that moment. I just want to scoop her up and tell her that it's okay, that I love her, and it doesn't matter about the spellings, the broken plate, the water all over the bathroom. The truth is that none of it was important – only I didn't know it at the time. My heart hurts when I think that I wasted precious momentsbeing cross with her, making her feel shame for something she'd done. I'm disgusted with myself for that, but those moments happen to every parent and you don't for a second think you are going to live to regret them. Whilst there were far more moments of love, connection, and laughter, it's those upsetting memories that stick fast in my mind. It's hard to explain how that feels and I hate myself for it.

I know Matt and I both feel an extra layer of guilt because Annaliese was adopted. It took us two years in the adoption process until that amazing day when we brought her home to live with us and from then on, we were the ones trusted to bring her up and to protect her. Our home should have been the best place she could grow up. I remember telling the doctor leading the team doing CPR that she was adopted, as if in some way that would make them try harder to keep her alive for us. I needed him to know how wanted she was, how precious she was after the years of waiting to become parents. We feel like we let her down, it's a heavy burden to live with.

There were many phone calls we had to make following that awful day and one of them was to social services. It was horrendous, and I couldn't believe we were telling them that our little girl had died. Of course, there was no judgement from them, but the judgement we place on ourselves is enough.

What have I learnt?

- Like anger, guilt is a wasted emotion – there's no real point to it, it changes nothing, however I've learnt that the guilt I live with isn't unusual. I know many bereaved parents feel the same and judge themselves as harshly as I do myself. Just knowing what I'm feeling is 'normal', is helpful.

- The feeling of isolation when you experience a life-changing event like this is enormous, suddenly you are different to 99% of people you know, and you think that you are the only ones in the world to feel like this. When you find your 'tribe' there's some relief in knowing that you aren't the only ones navigating your way through this dense jungle of emotions.

- I try not to dwell on the 'what ifs' - the truth is that they too, are futile. Nothing can change what has happened. We did the best that we could at the time, all our decisions were driven out of what we thought was the right thing to do and we listened to the professionals – what parent would do differently?

What can your support crew do to help?

- I'm not too sure there's much you can do apart from listen. The guilt someone feels is a very personal thing. I did have friends reassuring me that they would have done the same as me, maybe even less than me to try and help me 'go easy' on myself – but the truth is I need to come to terms with what happened on my own and if carrying some guilt about it is part of that, then so be it.

- I think encouraging the family to connect with people who have been through similar experiences (e.g., other bereaved parents) is a helpful and practical thing to do. Realising that the feelings you are experiencing are totally normal can be very reassuring.

- If you can persuade them to go for a walk with you every once in a while, that would be helpful. Just a short respite from focusing on their overwhelming feelings can make a difference.

Work

About 18 months before Annaliese died I was made redundant after working for a global organisation for 15 years. At the time I felt bereft, I'd loved working at the company and was good at what I did but the endless restructures caught up with me in the end. In hindsight I'm so thankful for that serendipitous timing. It meant that for the last 18 months of her life, I was at home and with Annaliese every day. At least I don't carry guilt for being away on business trips or 6am starts to get into the office early. I feel sad though that Matt was working long hours during that time (including night shifts) and he didn't see the kids much apart from weekends. I'm sure he feels the same.

When the bomb went off in our lives we were fortunate that neither of us had to stress about getting back to work. I had just set up a business in communications consulting and Matt was self-employed.

We didn't feel any pressure in that respect and could take the time we needed without having to update the boss. That was the good news. The bad news was that there was no income – a situation that we both reacted to very differently. Matt was immensely worried about how we would live, and I didn't worry about it at all. It felt like my brain just didn't have the space to take that on as well. Work, returning to work, employment and income is another area of life that is so different for every family coping with this depth of loss. For some, there is simply no option but to return to work. For others there may be a choice, but returning to work gives them some sort of normality or purpose and the distraction can be helpful.

For the past few years we have had very little income. I did some low-level freelancing which has been good for helping me to 'find myself' a little. More recently, I've come to a point where the time feels right to take on more and I've launched a business with a very close friend and ex-colleague and am so far loving the challenge and opportunity. It has taken time for me to feel ready, but I am hopeful for this venture. It's nice to be finding myself again.

Conversely, Matt has felt unable to return to work and I totally get that.

For him to go back would mean long hours and seeing very little of our son, which for him hasn't felt like the right thing to do. His last day at work was the day before Annaliese died. I called him to come home as I needed to take her to the doctor. That drive home for him holds painful memories and the songs he listened to on the way are still huge triggers. I'm grateful that my 25-year corporate career and our generally sensible attitude to finances allowed us the breathing space we needed. It's a very unusual way to live though.

Launching a business is a big and positive step, but I feel a lot less confident compared to the old me. This lack of confidence doesn't make sense, but from what I've seen and heard, it's very common amongst our 'club'. I've tried to understand why, and all I can come up with is that we now see the world as a totally unreliable place. We know that we are not in control of what happens. If we were, Annaliese would still be with us. Realising that makes you less confident about your place in the world. I also think we feel extremely self-conscious – something else I wasn't prepared for. This has definitely impacted my ability to 'put myself out there' for work.

For those of you who are returning to your job, I hope you find compassion and patience from those around you. Maybe some of the things in this book might help them to understand you better and what you now need.

What have I learnt?

- It's taken quite some time before I've been able to think about work. I was lucky to be able to allow myself a full year before I returned to any sort of paid work and even then, it was only a few hours a week from home.

- I've accepted that my brain is different now - at times I think of my grief as a brain injury – my neural pathways are irrevocably changed. I can still function, some days better than others, but not in the same way.

- I find remembering things harder, so I have to make several lists a day. Sometimes I find taking information in more challenging and on a 'bad' day I just accept that I'm not up to it and do something to 'rest' my brain.

- I spent 25 years working in busy corporate environments, that's who I was, so this slower pace of life is a big change for me, but that's okay. I have learnt to do what feels right, and I've found some different ways to make a bit of money (through my creative work) which would never have had the space to flourish before.

- It is possible to make great progress – I recently delivered a day of training with my business partner to a room full of people and I enjoyed it immensely. I would never have believed I was capable of something like that in the early years after Annaliese's death – so I guess the point is – in time, you might be able to find yourself again.

What can your work support crew do to help?

- Be generous with your compassionate leave policies – losing and saying goodbye to your child at their funeral isn't something you recover from easily or quickly or ever. If you can give people a decent amount of paid time off (6 months or more), that's the biggest, most practical thing you can do to help in the first instance.
- Listen to your employee and help them feel more in control of their return to work. Are you able to make changes to the role to ensure the bereaved parent isn't under too much pressure? Can you make sure they don't have too much public/customer facing time at first? If you can be flexible in this way, do it - they will be so thankful.
- 'Brief' their colleagues on the new plan so that your bereaved employee doesn't have to explain it themselves. Ask colleaguesnot to overwhelm your employee with kindness - it will make us cry every single time. Be understanding that sometimes

their reactions / behaviour might be different to normal. Just being aware and accepting this, is immensely helpful.

- Don't be afraid to mention their child's name – you won't be reminding them; you will be remembering them - and that's precious for us all.

- Think proactively about times of the year that are likely to be extra difficult for them – birthdays and anniversaries are obvious, but don't forget that Mother's & Father's Day will be painful too. Easter and Christmas are likely to be times when they feel extra sensitive and maybe the start of a new school year if their child was still at school. Ask them to tell you when they need extra space / time off so that you can both plan for it.

- Be patient – this sort of grief lives with you forever and can overwhelm us at the most unexpected moments. We might hear a particular song on the radio, listen to someone talk about their family or see a child wearing a similar piece of clothing. The 'triggers' are everywhere, so please be patient.

- Get comfortable with emotions. Someone once told me that tears are pain leaving the body, and I get great comfort from that. If someone needs a few tears or a deep sob, just let them. You don't need to say much (if anything), they are not looking for solutions, just be there and hold their pain.

- A phased return to work is something that I know a lot of people have found helpful – starting a couple of half days and gradually building up to their normal working pattern.

The Person You Are Now

(The Side Effects of Grief/Finding Purpose)

This is such a big one. You have no idea that the death of your child is going to fundamentally change you as a person. It took a while for me to realise this and accept it. Obviously in those first few weeks you are still in shock and literally just muddle your way through what needs to be done. The loss of self-confidence was, and still is, a big one for me. Over the months, it became clear that I couldn't handle the things I used to take in my stride. I literally lost the person I used to be, and it was terrifying. I was three months shy of my 50th birthday when Annaliese died, so learning to accept the different version of myself was hard as I'd had nearly five decades of being my previous self.

I became awkward in social situations; I lost my ability to multi-task and I felt so self-conscious of myself and of our diminished family unit. I would walk down the street hoping not to see anyone I knew. I kept my eyes low, looking at the pavement slabs, and wore headphones - a clear signal that I wasn't up for connecting. It was a stark change in my feelings and behaviour. I'm gradually learning to cope better, but I'm still changed and accepting that is part of the healing, I think.

I want to talk about anger. I would never have classed myself as an angry person previously. I think I'd had flashes of it when, for example, I couldn't get pregnant and all my friends were happily cooing over their babies and when my Mum died aged sixty-two in a matter of weeks, but generally speaking, I wasn't prone to the red mist. Boy did I get to know it in the months following Annaliese's death. I was angry at so many things and it's such a destructive emotion. I was angry at life (how could this happen?), myself (why couldn't I keep her safe?), the doctors (why didn't they save her?), her friends (why were they all still alive?), my friends (how dare they moan about their struggles with their kids?), our families (why didn't they understand us better?) The unfairness of it all totally consumed me. I'm grateful that I never felt angry with Matt or our son. They were in this mess with me too, we were a team and we had to find a way to survive together.

I wonder if some of those who were previously close to me found this new, damaged, angry version of myself hard to cope with? I suspect some thought I was too 'obsessed' with my daughter's death, that I was slightly delusional by continuing to include her name on any cards or letters I sent (I still do), that it wasn't 'healthy' for me to still say, if asked, 'I've got two children, but unfortunately my daughter died'. They are, of course, entitled to their opinions but I guess this is the chance to give mine. Count yourself lucky indeed if you can't understand or accept the way I was behaving, the things I was doing or the way I was talking. Be grateful that you aren't me, spending every single hour for the rest of my life missing my little girl, wishing she was back in my arms, being given the chance to grow up and have her future. I am finding a way to live my life; I don't cry every day now, but I do think about her all the time. It's impossible not to.

It feels uncomfortable to admit this, but I do think there are some positive things emerging from this new version of me. On days where I'm able to reject the anger and contain the raw emotion, I am now someone who realises the trivial nature of much that happens in our daily lives. Most stuff that goes on really isn't important. It's not life and death. I worry less that the kitchen floor looks like a barnyard (thanks to our furry family member), I don't fret so much about the future because I know it's not guaranteed. I've become a little more selfish which I'm counting as a good thing, and I take far more notice of the simple things in life – a beautiful blue sky, the sound of birds tweeting from the hedges surrounding my garden, the gorgeous feeling of the warm sun on my face through my bedroom window as I listen to ocean waves on my Alexa. I'm better able to appreciate the moment, to be in the moment more than I was before. My world is SO much smaller and I'm okay with that. I am very choosy about who I spend my time with because I need to feel safe and supported much of the time. I try to avoid situations where I know I'm likely to get triggered - it's called self-protection. Though this new version of me worries less about the future, I need to clarify that this doesn't stretch to my son. I worry about his future constantly, and I can't see a time when that will ever change.

Given that I've not done much paid work since Annaliese died, I've had the time to indulge and develop my creative side which I've absolutely loved. I've spent hours painting, printing, drawing, and it feels like a connection to her. She and I used to sit around our big kitchen table doing colouring together, listening to Christmas songs in the middle of summer and I think of her often when I'm sat there working on a project. I've rediscovered my passion for reading though it took me 18 months or so before I could concentrate enough to cope with a book, and now I have so much pleasure from curling up somewhere with my latest page-turner.

During the pandemic my old university housemates and I set up regular Zoom calls to reconnect and decided we should start a book club. It's been fantastic to enjoy books that I'd never have chosen myself and more than that, to be able to chat and laugh with three dear friends. Despite meeting them over thirty years ago, these friends continue to be an important part of my life. The Collins Road book club was a wonderful tonic.

What have I learnt?

- To accept that I'm different now and that's okay. I'm still me, just a new version of me. It takes some getting used to but accepting and adapting to this new me has brought some element of relief.
- Not to feel guilty about the 'positives'. Obviously, I'd give them all up in a moment if it meant I could have Annaliese back, but that's not an option, so I'm choosing to find things to be grateful for where I can. It seems a healthier way to live for me personally.
- Anger achieves nothing, the only person it really has an impact on is me so I'm learning (very slowly) to let go of it whenever I can. When I do manage it, it feels liberating, so I'm going to continue to work hard on this one.

What can your support crew do to help?

- Be patient and make allowances for any changed behaviour or demeanour you might (will) see. Getting to grips with the fact that everyone grieves differently is like a lightbulb moment. Once you understand this you can accept that however someone is behaving, it's how they need to be right now. Allow them that moment.

- Forgive any bad behaviour, angry outbursts, uncharacteristic sharpness – you have it in your gift to do this. We don't mean it, it's just part of the process, part of coming to terms with the changed reality and all that brings.

- Don't distance yourself because a terrible thing has happened. As the weeks, months, and years progress, just be there for your friend or family member. There may be times when it feels like they are rejecting or avoiding you, and that may be the case, but it will only be momentary. Give them time, a few more weeks and then do something kind. Send them a card to let them know you are there, that you are thinking about them and maybe share a memory you have of their child. I always love it when people share their memories of Annaliese with me. Supporting a bereaved parent is hard work, it takes a huge amount of love, compassion, and patience but if you can do it, you are indeed a precious person in their lives.

- Observe and enjoy some of the new elements of a bereaved parent's personality. Accept them as they are now and try to resist thinking about how they used to be 'before' or thinking too far into the future. Here and now is what matters - embrace it.

A Different Perspective

What it feels like for your friends. Here's a piece of writing by one of my best friends, to see things through her eyes.

She's gone. I will remember those words forever. Annaliese was my friend and Clare and I became friends because of Annaliese. Because she decided I was one of her special people and, come rain or shine, she made my world brighter.

Anneliese's death caused a ripple effect of grief across our small community. People felt helpless and lost, unsure of what they could or should do. Everyone wanted to help but no-one knew how. A few of us spent the first days in shifts at the house so that Clare and Matt weren't on their own. I remember us not wanting to leave each other.

I collected Annaliese's little brother from school on the day she died and had to hold onto my emotions and try to be normal for him. Looking back, I'm not sure how I did that. I remember arriving at the hospital and seeing Clare and Matt physically and emotionally broken, numb with shock. Together with another friend we called every parent in Annaliese's class. I recall saying over and over again that she had died. It was like an out of body experience and I was in robot mode. The brief distraction of these calls was almost welcome. Being practical helped to hold back the emotion. Everyone behaved differently, all with shock and sadness but some had no words, others asked questions, and there was a diverse range of immediate thoughts which I think is an indicator of how differently we all react to loss and grief. Some people didn't know what to say to Clare and Matt so would ask me for advice, hoping I'd be able to offer them the right words. There's a compulsion to try and fix what is broken and to make it better. Faced with a situation though that is not only unfixable but unfathomable, a situation which contravenes the natural order of generational passing - renders people frozen, uncomfortable and outside of anything they've experienced before. The natural reaction is to avoid the awkwardness and the pain because sitting in that space with someone is to sit in darkness and pain too. Most people are simply not able to do that.

Avoidance never seemed like a choice for me - I was living and breathing the sadness with Clare and Matt. You might ask why? Because I wanted to support and help them, but selfishly, I lived and breathed it for me too. By being close to Clare, Matt and their little boy, I was also staying close to Annaliese, and that meant I felt I was doing something for her, for them, rather than sitting helplessly on the sidelines.

When you don't know what to say that's okay. You don't have to say or do anything. There is nothing within your power that can fix what has happened so the bravery comes from sitting in that powerless space, silencing your own need to help and just being available to meet your loved one where they are. It could be in silence, in tears, in memories, in anger, or in fear. I felt lucky that I was emotionally able to do that. I was certainly in the minority.

Walking into the house for the first time after Annaliese's death was surreal. Clare and Matt were still in the hospital and had not been home. Seeing Annaliese's clothes on the airer and her Hama beads on the table – time stood still. Everything collapsed for a moment before distraction kicked in and I realised that I had to be practical - Clare and Matt needed things to be done.

Going to see Annaliese in the funeral home is something that will stay with me forever. She looked like herself, her beautiful face and her Cinderella dress, but she was cold and still. She was gone and the emotional impact of that felt all consuming. As painful as it was though, I was privileged that I got to say goodbye, I got to release the emotion I was holding and I felt honoured that Clare and Matt trusted me to visit their daughter so that I could help them decide if they should visit her too.

Writing the poem to read at Annaliese's funeral was in equal parts sad yet cathartic as it allowed me to express my grief by remembering her through the words on the page and sharing that with the congregation who sat in tangible disbelief and sadness. Annaliese's funeral was one of the saddest days of my life. There had been plenty of sad days between her death and the funeral, but for me, that day was the hardest.

The inquest – this was just awful – I can't really articulate the weight of sadness, pain and anger that I felt watching Clare and Matt go through this, re-shattering their world with every sentence spoken. It was almost like an out of body experience and it felt impossible to believe that we were there because Annaliese was dead.

Clare and Matt have walked different paths of grief over the years but they have stayed alongside each other, like each had an outstretched arm in the darkness, their fingertips still connected. Slowly they have interlocked fingers, linked arms and found their way back to the same path. They are changed people, their son too, they are a changed family, but they are the strongest, bravest, most resilient, wonderful family I know.

To meet someone's need in immediate, intense grief is to take their lead. Try not to drag them out of the darkness because you want them to get there. Be patient, meet them where they are and they will let you know what they need. You can tell by how they behave, be it silent, sad, angry, reminiscent, practical - whatever that need is, just share that space with them and show reassurance that however they are feeling is okay. And stick around. If you have been a part of their grieving process, don't pull away when everything practical is done and emotions have calmed just a little, this is the time they need you most. The outside world seems to go back to normal, but their world is still in fragments on the floor. That is when they need you to steady their walk, remember their pain and remember the person who is lost.

I send a kiss or a heart emoji to Clare every time she pops into my head just to let her know I am thinking of her. I call her when I have a memory of Annaliese and I let her know if I do or experience something that I think Annaliese would have enjoyed. I let Clare know because she wants to know, she wants Annaliese's memory to be very much alive and that means *saying* her name, *writing* hername in every card and *remembering her*.

Who she was to us and the unforgettable impact she had on our lives.

A Poem For Annaliese

Written by Alex and Claire (and read by them at the funeral)

So many words to choose from
But none that seem quite enough
To describe your wonder and our sadness
So Leasie, you've made this job real tough.

All of us here today
Shared the honour of loving you
And although overwhelmed by our loss
We feel the love of you shine through.

Standing in line at pick up time
Scanning the playground for us privileged ones,
To scream our names and come running
With hugs warmer than a million suns

Once the hugs were done
The buggies were your goal
Those handles that you'd help to push
And enrich the driveway stroll

We shared the beauty of your world
When you gifted a pebble or feather
You touched so many of our lives
And we will be grateful to you forever

Your cheeky go on the rollover bars
While everyone stood in line
Your determination to do what made you happy
That's what made you shine

You were a force to be reckoned with
An unpredictable masterpiece
You could not be persuaded
Our strong and beautiful Annaliese

So many individual memories
That out of nowhere we would find
Soft and warm your little hand
Around ours would be entwined

Forever remembered in your blue spotty hat
And a smile that lit up the world
Your infectious enthusiasm for the joy of life
It inspired us all dear girl

You loved all the animals
And cared for your friends
The tender heart inside you
That could always make amends

Every picture drawn with a smile
And great big tick WELL DONE
You lived your life as you drew it Leasie
You gave it your all. And then some.

A princess you were born to be
And OH how you played the part
Dancing and singing in your kitchen
Etching memories on your family's hearts

On your rope swing in the garden
Or sofa snuggles with your blankee
Home is where you were happiest
And where your memory will always be

You took such pride in your creations
Out of Lego and Hama beads
And to deviate from the instructions
Not in your wildest dreams

How you loved the wonder of the stars
Shining bright up in the sky
Annaliese you are the brightest star of all
Forever safe in mummas lullaby.

"Alex, you're a cheeky monkey,"
That's what you would say
Leasie your presence in my world
Would illuminate my cloudiest day

Always one last cuddle goodbye
When we were getting in our car
The last stone sits on my windowsill
My most precious gift by far

You were just too special for this world
And that's why you had to go
To have had you for the time we did
We've been blessed, that we know.

~~~
~~~

A Few Years On…

It seems somehow impossible that it's been over four years since I've seen, held, cuddled, and kissed my little girl. Despite having my feet firmly on the ground and being a pragmatic person, I still have difficulty believing that it happened. To her, to us, at all. I've recounted the sequence of events many times over those years – it's almost like an out of body experience. I know the facts; I can visualise her last 24 hours almost moment by moment, but I still haven't reached complete acceptance yet. I'm told it will come and at this point I'm able to believe it, which is something I was unable to do for the first couple of years. I know we will survive this catastrophic loss. I know I am learning to live with the hole she has left in our lives. I'm able to enjoy myself - mostly. I'm able to really laugh at things again and I look forward to seeing certain people or places.

But, and it's a hefty *but*, I have this deep, unwavering sadness within me that at times threatens to overwhelm. There's a permanent fracture in our family unit which will never be repaired. I see the sadness and despair on both Matt and my son's faces and it absolutely breaks my heart. Of course, Annaliese should be here, creating havoc, complaining about homework, telling me how unfair it is that she hasn't got an iPhone or social media account yet, experiencing her first year of senior school, annoying her brother, giving us big hugs, wanting me to sing our special lullaby at bedtime, colouring in at the kitchen table and watching hours and hours of Disney +. But she isn't and despite the huge loss, we are moving forwards as a family and trying to build the best future we can.

After months of discussions and assessments, we have been lucky enough to adopt again. Another son, a little brother to our other two. It feels somewhat surreal and of course emotional, but I am looking forward to helping him get to know the big sister that he'll never meet. And I'm full of hope that enabling the boys to grow up together will make us all feel happier.

I will miss her physical presence until the day I die, but I still feel her with me somehow. Annaliese remains such a big part of my life and the connections I have with her are, and always have been, meaningful. She is my only daughter, the one I had always yearned for. She is the toddler that introduced me to motherhood and whom I fell hopelessly in love with quickly and without hesitation.

Thank you, Annaliese, for everything. I'm proud to be your Mummy. Your death left me broken and directionless but somehow I kept going. I can recognise that in part this experience has left me a better, more balanced, more accepting, and less judgemental mother and person. That, I believe, is your final gift to me.

I wish it had been different but I will love you endlessly and I'm so grateful for the few years we had together.

I will see you again one day munchkin and I cannot wait to feel the weight of you in my arms as you knock me over with one of your legendary flying hugs.

Acknowledgements

Firstly, to my best friend and soulmate Matt. We've bumbled our way through these past few years trying our absolute best to support each other and cope with our grief. You are a wonderful person and I'm so glad to have you by my side. I'm sorry the way life has panned out – it's not what we expected – but seeing you become a Daddy to Annaliese was one of the happiest times of my life. Your connection to her was immediate and you both knew it. She loved you unconditionally and I know you felt the same. Thank you for being you.

To our son – you are an amazing boy who, for a young child, has had far too much to cope with. You are brave, kind and loving at your best, but can be angry, frustrated and scared too, all of which is understandable. I love you always and forever. Your sister would be so proud of you, as are both Daddy and I. We know you are going to be a great big brother too.

To my friends Alex and Claire – you've stood alongside me every single step of the way since that fateful day. You've been unwavering in your support, unconditional with your love and totally accepting of how I need to be. I truly believe that there were times when you kept me going, and I also believe Annaliese brought you into my life for a reason. I know you miss her deeply too and in you, I know I have friends for life. Thank you for everything, including keeping her memory alive and your love for our son. I am a better person for having both of you in my life.

To 'Aunty' Sue – we've known each other for decades and you have become such an important and treasured part of our lives. Thank you for everything - your kindness with Annaliese and her brothers, your thoughtfulness and understanding of us - you make our family better just being around and I'm thankful for you every day.

To the fellow bereaved parents that I've met through *The Compassionate Friends.* You've become a part of my life and have been there for me when I've needed to vent, talk about Annaliese, ask questions, share photos and just be my true self - however ugly that has been. In you I've found hope, inspiration, determination, honesty, friendship, kindness and understanding. I know we would all rather not know each other – but I'm proud to stand with you.

To Emmalene – thank you for your legal guidance and support, for fighting hard for what was right in honour of our daughter.

To Helen – your kindness and thoughtfulness during the weeks and months following Annaliese's death will always be remembered. Thank you for the care and compassion you showed us all and for keeping the memory of her alive in school whilst you were there.

To Anne-Marie – thank you for the patience, kindness and support you have shown us all as a family. You've helped Matt and I learn how to better parent our beautiful son, who is dealing with the most horrendous trauma. You've listened, shown compassion, and never made us feel judged or self-conscious.

To Jo – thank you for supporting our son, for understanding him and helping us to believe it's going to be okay.

To Louise – thank you for your medical expertise and support in the lead up to and at the inquest. Your kindness and advice meant so much to both of us at that very stressful time.

To David – for pushing me to ask the hard questions, for being by our side at the inquest and for introducing me to Matt, you truly changed my life for the better.

To Kate and Lyndon – for taking my middle of the night calls during that first week, for letting me cry and talk nonsense when I needed to.

To the rest of our support crew - Clare, Gemma, Dee and many others. Thank you for simply being there when we needed you.

To Paul – thank you for your words of comfort, for giving me hope and for the wonderful moments you and Annaliese had together. Remembering your amazing son Aidan.

To Jenny – thanks for the forensic proof reading.

To AnnMarie – thank you for your endless patience and encouragement. I'd never have got there without your help – and now I know what an Oxford comma is too!

To Michael Heppell and the Write That Book 2021/22 groups – thank you for making this book a reality. I thought I might want to write about my experiences but never really knew how to start. Thank you for your positivity, encouragement and guidance. You are brilliant!

To Annaliese – for everything you were and everything you have made me.

xxx

Helpful Resources

Children's books

The Invisible String – Patrice Karst

Badger's Parting Gifts – Susan Varley

Where Are You: A Child's Book About Loss – Laura Olivieri

When Someone Very Special Dies: Children Can Learn to Cope with Grief – Marge Heegaard

Muddles, Puddles and Sunshine – Diana Crossley

The Memory Tree – Britta Teckentrup

Michael Rosen's Sad Book – Michael Rosen

Bereavement groups and charities

There's so much support out there. Search on the internet for relevant organisations and their contact details, but here are a few I'd recommend:

The Compassionate Friends - for parents, siblings and grandparents.

Winston's Wish - who support children and young people after the death of a parent or sibling.

Child Bereavement UK - for children, young people, parents and families.

Cruse Bereavement Care - free care and bereavement counselling to people suffering from grief.

The Good Grief Trust - help and hope in one place.

Grief Encounter - supporting bereaved children and young people

Author Biography

Clare came to motherhood later in life (following fertility challenges and the long adoption process) but got there eventually. Before the devastating loss of her daughter Annaliese, she had a successful career as a communications professional with a full, enjoyable family and social life. In learning to live with her grief as a bereaved parent, Clare has found a different approach to life focusing on the things and the people that bring her joy, taking one day at a time and remembering her little girl every step of the way. She lives in a male dominated household, with her partner, sons and Labradoodle Gus Gus! And Always Annaliese x is her first book which she was inspired to write after joining Michael Heppell's Write That Book Masterclass group.